T0072403

Honoring Gifts, Rising to Challenges

Honoring Gifts, Rising to Challenges

A Guide to Fostering Naturally Confident Learners

Judy Donovan

HONORING GIFTS, RISING TO CHALLENGES
A GUIDE TO FOSTERING NATURALLY CONFIDENT LEARNERS

iUniverse books may be ordered through booksellers or by contacting:

iUniverse
1663 Liberty Drive
Bloomington, IN 47403
www.iuniverse.com
1-800-Authors (1-800-288-4677)

ISBN: 978-1-4917-4544-1 (sc)
ISBN: 978-1-4917-4548-9 (e)

Print information available on the last page.

iUniverse rev. date: 05/22/2015

Table of Contents

Section 1: The Idea 1
Section 2: Laying the Foundation 4
Section 3: The Lesson 30
Section 4: Creativity 61
Section 5: Materials and Ideas for In-Depth Work 69
Section 6: Additional Material for Teachers 84
Section 7: Alumni Perspectives 104
Section 8: Comments from Teachers 108
Section 9: The Journals 111

Dedication

This work is dedicated to Anthony Piazza and his mother, Rosa Trujillo. It is also for all students who might receive these ideas into their hearts and use them to achieve their true potential with natural confidence and joy.

Introduction

The information in this book is presented primarily as a guide for teachers of children ages 5 to 12. Yet, it is meaningful for anyone who has ever struggled with a challenge or felt ashamed by a lack of understanding in any aspect of his or her learning. It addresses the inner dialogue of negative comparison that can take hold when ranking one's own learning progress in a harsh and comparative tone. It can act as an inoculation or antidote to the sometimes thoughtless and hurtful comments of classmates. It can lead to a natural confidence that is underpinned by a realistic and honest understanding of one's own gifts and challenges.

The "lessons" in this journal were inspired by the idea that there must be a way to better protect the child's right to learn at the speed and in the style that is most suited to each. In tandem with this thought is that the emotional climate of the classroom as a whole must be strengthened so that it is an encouraging atmosphere for everyone. To me, this meant dramatically re-educating and awakening the sensitivity of all my students. It is my hope that these practices will not only make many classrooms safer places to learn, but that as the children themselves absorb these ideas, they will ultimately become the guardians of their own emotional safety as they continue learning throughout their lives.

The Gifts and Challenges vocabulary is also an essential tool for parents to ensure that their child's natural eagerness to learn with confident curiosity is kept alive all through the school years. When challenges are encountered, parents can use the Gifts and Challenges vocabulary to help guide their child through these emotional moments in a positive and uplifting manner. If a child's gifts begin to foster a one-upmanship attitude, a more balanced approach can be simply and respectfully explained.

The premise is that we all have the potential to "exercise our full powers along the lines of excellence" (Cassell, 1988) if we know the educational facts of life. These facts are offered in simple and easily applicable lessons in the Gifts and Challenges material. The inspiration is that all children can be taught these basic truths and then choose to live that way, in a balanced and joyful approach to learning. This natural confidence is our birthright.

It is painful to witness anyone go through the internal anguish of self-doubt about their abilities, especially when facing a challenge, but also when hiding the light of their gifts through fear of being thought of as too self-aggrandizing. Having seen this struggle, you may have wished for a key to free that person to fulfill their greatest potential with joy, confidence, and enthusiasm.

The principles taught in Gifts and Challenges can provide an important link to reaching that emotional freedom and natural confidence we are all searching for. They teach that:

- Everyone has gifts and challenges.

- There is no one who has all gifts and no one who has all challenges.

- Gifts are to be honored.

- It is natural to be excited and happy when exercising a gift and natural to want to share that gift.

- Challenges are to be recognized and accepted.

- It is human nature to want to avoid a challenge, but with friendly support we can rise to our challenges, practice to get better, and then share our triumphs or breakthroughs.

This material has been taught and implemented for more than 15 years in a Montessori elementary classroom, yet it can be applied in any school. My students have been integral in the development of the material and have repeatedly asked for these lessons each year. They have incorporated the vocabulary and the ideas into their daily lives in the classroom. They have compassionately and matter-of-factly shared their understandings and encouragement with each other.

It is my hope that these ideas will spread to your classrooms, your homes, and your minds. I have experienced how invaluable they are in my work with children. They have the potential to be helpful in family dynamics. Perhaps they can act as a spring-board to repairing any damage you may have personally undergone through your own school experience. It's possible they can shed some light on confidence and self-doubt issues. But certainly, the understanding of these simple principles holds great promise toward freeing each of us to be our best selves and thereby make a contribution to the human family that would inspire us all.

Judy Donovan

Section 1: The Idea

The Vision for Gifts and Challenges

The essence of this lesson has to do with revealing to children the simple insights needed for self understanding and self acceptance as learners. The vision is to make our classroom communities a safe place to be "in the process of learning." The program is designed to foster natural confidence in all students, at all levels of ability, while they are on their way to becoming their true best selves.

Begun in a working Montessori classroom in 1998, the ideas were inspired by the children themselves. The project has continued to evolve over the years with the input of both children and teachers.

This lesson is a way into the heart of how children can begin to think of themselves as powerful learners, whether they are doing an activity that comes naturally or struggling to understand and perform a difficult task. It is a set of basic ideas about what is common for all human beings in the exploration of their own education. In this approach, education does not merely include the academic subjects, but also encompasses creativity, kinesthetic abilities, people skills, virtues, and the world of nature.

Through careful teacher modeling, the children are helped to recognize their own gifts, and to accept as natural, their own challenges. The lesson begins as a story, expands into a day of exercising the students' gifts, and another of practicing their challenges. It continues throughout the year with discussions, role playing, variations on the theme (including children's input), as well as spontaneous applications which arise organically in the daily life of the classroom. The terms "gifts and challenges" are woven into our daily vocabulary, and by doing this, the children are remembering and applying this to their understanding of themselves and each other. It is a gradual infusion, and the children take it in as they are able. In turn, this contributes to the emotional safety of the classroom. The children learn to honor their own gifts and to admire and encourage the gifts they see in their classmates. They also gain insight into how to accept their own challenges. They begin to practice the special language and technique of supporting another in facing a challenge. This creates a naturally unifying atmosphere in the classroom, which grows from that "aha" feeling that we are all in this together. From that idea, comes the freedom to ask for help without shame. Equally important, it fosters the rare ability to offer help with the true humility of understanding that you yourself will need help with a challenge at another time.

When you are confident about your gifts and accepting of your challenges, you are freed to become a more compassionate human being.

We are all essentially "works in progress." The realization that as teachers and learners we can all make an invaluable contribution to each other and ultimately to the world by being and accepting exactly who we are, whatever our stage of learning, is the true gift of this work.

Original Inspiration

As a Montessori teacher, I was inspired by a young student in my classroom named Anthony to present this lesson that came to be called Gifts and Challenges. Anthony and I had already spent lots of time together, since his mother and I were good friends, and I was privileged to be considered one of his "aunties." One evening, his mom called me to say that he was very upset and crying about his homework. Another child had told him he really should be in a higher numbered reading workbook. My reaction to this was very strong, not only for Anthony's sake, but also because of a core belief in making my classroom a safe place for all children and their individual learning rates and styles.

Each year, my staff and I had worked anew on creating a non-competitive atmosphere, using role playing, class meetings, and positive language to help the students learn how to encourage each other and to feel safe themselves about their own learning.

So, I was discouraged to see that all our "talks and techniques" appeared to be ineffective in the face of one thoughtless comment. And now, my young student was brought to tears in my supposedly safe classroom. I got on the phone and spent several minutes reminding Anthony of what he already knew how to do well and assured him that he deserved all the time he needed to complete his reading workbook. Anthony seemed somewhat comforted, but I was not. When I got off the phone I was angry and thought, "This cannot happen! Not in my room!" It was already late—a school night, so I prepared for bed and began a night of serious tossing and turning. I kept replaying classroom scenarios, looking for a way I had not tried yet. How could my students be reached on this critical issue? Finally, at about 4:30 in the morning some ideas began to come—lots of ideas! Writing them down, three or four pages later I realized I would be late for work if I didn't stop right away.

Arriving at school, more notes were written, and I resolved to speak about these ideas as soon as all the children arrived. In short, the children would be receiving a "talk" called Gifts and Challenges. In truth, I was anxious about taking this risk with my class. "Would they even know what I was talking about? Would it be too much for them to absorb? Would Anthony himself understand what I meant and be able to take it to heart?" In spite of the doubts, I put some of the material from the notes up on the whiteboard to be available as a visual aid.

As the children began filing in, I jokingly whispered to my assistant Mel that I was about to do something out of the ordinary at Circle, which could be a big mistake or really exciting. I said that I definitely would want her to be present while I embarked on this unusual experiment. My talk began as a serious event. I cleared my throat and began reading from my "script," which was completely out of character for me. With a passionate tone of voice, there was an air of drama to the scene. I'm sure all this seemed quite strange to my students and maybe that's why they gave me their complete attention from the beginning. It began with a story... You will find this story and how it is presented in the "Lesson" chapter.

The following chapter will help get your children ready to receive the lesson in an atmosphere of respect and cooperation.

Section 2: Laying the Foundation

In order to create a safe place for sharing feelings and being honest about our own gifts and challenges, a short series of lessons and talks is introduced at the beginning of the year. This will help establish emotional literacy and build an atmosphere of mutual respect in the classroom community.

The ideas in this section are an integral part of most Montessori classrooms. They are included here for use as a possible blueprint for those classrooms which have not already established these kinds of systems.

The following "emotional literacy" tools are essential. They are presented here in hopes that these or similar ground rules will be firmly in place before introducing the Gifts and Challenges lesson. A framework such as this will give the lesson the best chance for remaining a positive on-going contribution to the emotional safety of your classroom.

Tools for Creating Emotional Safety in the Classroom

Feelings Vocabulary

At the beginning of the school year, it is essential to establish a common emotional vocabulary for the students to begin utilizing as they communicate during class meetings, problem solving, and in their daily conversations. In order to teach the language of feelings in an attention catching and concrete manner, a Feelings Wheel is used, based on the poster from "How Does Your Cat Feel?" This is a copyrighted product from How Do You Feel Today? Productions, www.howdoyoufeeltoday.com. (Permission was given to show a picture of the wheel, but it is not for use in copying.) Each face has an emotion word printed under the cat's depiction of that feeling. For the wheel, the faces that would be most appropriate for children and our teaching purposes have been chosen. There are many varieties of feelings charts on the market, but there has been a great response from the children toward the cat faces, so that is the source for all the feelings materials in the classroom.

In the lesson, draw a cat face on the board and have the children guess which feeling the cat is representing. The emotions are divided into two categories—Comfortable and Uncomfortable, which is an idea borrowed from the Joy Wilt book called *Handling Your Ups and Downs-A Kid's Guide to Emotions.* When we do the activity, two emotions are demonstrated from each category. This lesson is repeated several times during the first few weeks of school and then interspersed as needed. This has proven to be a very effective way to help children express a wide range of feelings with accuracy and understanding.

The Feelings Wheel Lesson

1. Gather the children in front of the Whiteboard. Show the Feelings Wheel, which many returning students have seen. Remind the students of the wheel's use in problem solving and state that today we are going to play a guessing game with the cat faces.

2. Write the labels Comfortable and Uncomfortable in two separate columns on the board. Draw a cat face on the Uncomfortable side. Start with "nervous," as many students can relate to feeling nervous about coming to school if it's their first time in your classroom.

3. Allow the children to make guesses as to what the feeling might be. (If drawing is not a choice, enlarge each face without the labels and tape one of them up under the category as you progress through the game.)

4. As the children guess incorrectly, encourage them by repeating their feelings word and then something like, "that's close" or "no, but good guess" to keep the positive momentum going. You are working to expand everyone's vocabulary range between the two extremes of happy and sad.

5. After a moderate number of guesses, you can give the answer as well as a personal example of when you felt that way. Then sing the song (see pg. 10). Invite children to share their own examples for a particular emotion and then repeat the song after all child examples are shared.

Needs Vocabulary

Another early lesson is the Introduction of the Needs Wheel. The list of needs comes from the book called *The Compassionate Classroom*, 2004, by Sura Hart and Victoria Kindle Hodson. This Wheel has been designed by adding icons for each Need on the Wheel (see photo, page 9). The icons can also be drawn on the board. Individual large cards for each need could also be created for easier reference during a group lesson. In talking about the Needs Wheel, there is a great opportunity to emphasize the commonality of needs by giving examples yourself or by asking for class participation to make this part of the lesson come alive.

The four general categories of the needs are: Physical, Feelings, Learning, and Inspirational.

Needs List

This list is adapted from The Compassionate Classroom. I have labeled Categories of Needs in simple language so that children can more easily think about their needs. When using the Needs Wheel the four different categories are color-coded by tracing over the spokes of the wheel with a colored marker. The categories are Physical, Feelings, Learning, and Inspirational. Of course more can be added or substituted as you see fit. You can involve your children in generating the list which would help to make the experience their own and more meaningful.

Physical Needs: Food, Exercise, Play/Fun, Physical Safety, Shelter, Touch, and Rest

Feelings: Belonging, Emotional Safety, Kindness, Respect, Sharing of Gifts, Trust, Support, Acceptance, Love, and Appreciation

Learning: Knowledge, Concentration, Acknowledgment, Achievement, Challenges, Creativity, and Choice

Inspirational: Beauty, Contact with Nature, Harmony, Inspiration, Order, and Peace

Ideally, the Needs Wheel is used as one step in the problem solving process. In this step, the children are asked to identify the need they were trying to meet regarding the problem situation.

Needs cards have also been created as an activity for exploring this vocabulary.

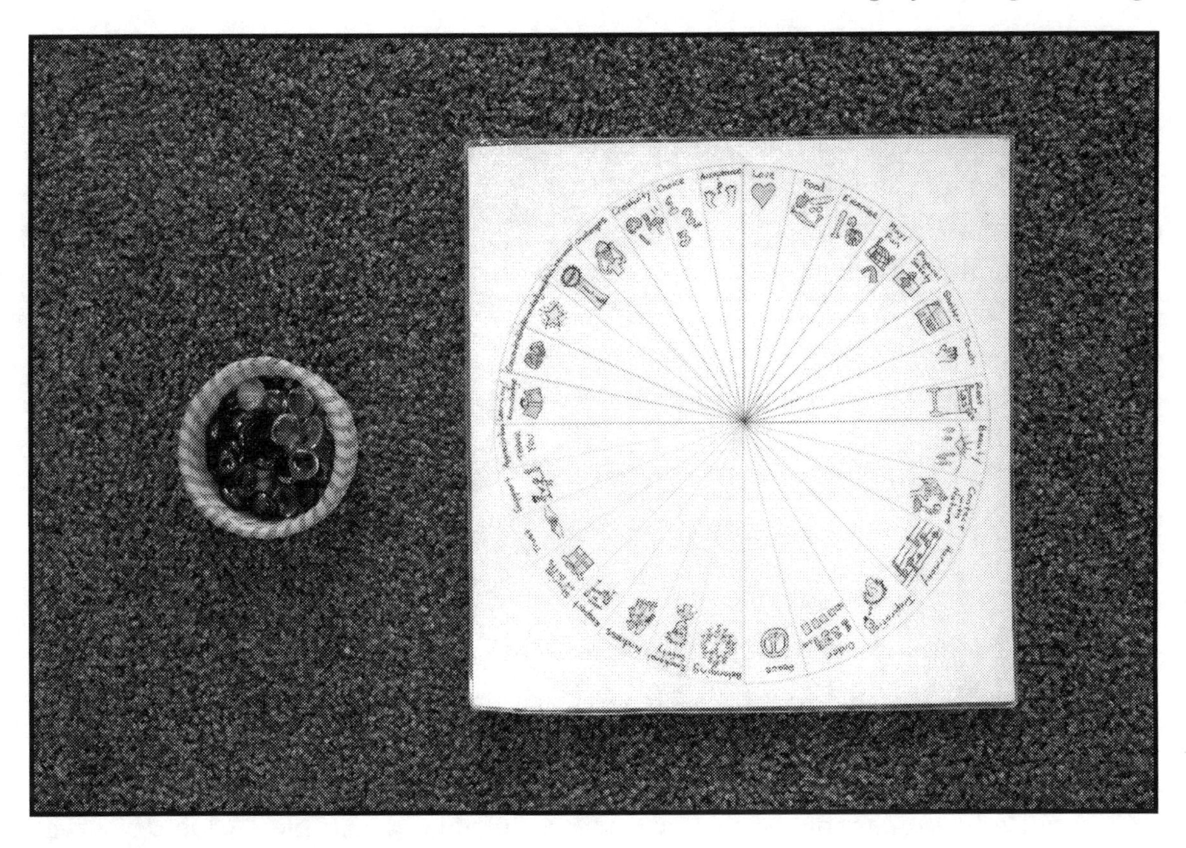

The Needs Wheel Lesson

1. Gather the children in front of the whiteboard. Show the Needs Wheel. State that even though we usually use this wheel for problem solving, it can also help us to learn about the many needs that all people have.

2. Write the label for one type of need on the board. The types are: Physical, Feelings, Learning, and Inspirational. Choose one from the Physical category first, as it seems more concrete and relatable for the children. Draw the need on the board or use large pre-made cards illustrating each unlabeled need.

3. Allow the children to guess what need the picture represents since that is what engages them in the activity. You might use the need for rest and say that you feel best in school when you have had enough rest. Invite the students to talk about how it feels when they don't get enough rest, and share your own story.

4. Teach several needs from the first category in the first session, then go on to "Feelings" needs until you have covered all four categories. This will usually take four or five sessions to complete. Showcase this lesson frequently at the beginning of the year and then interject it throughout the year.

Mistakes Vocabulary

This lesson is designed to help make the classroom safe for healthy risk-taking, promote tolerance for transparency in the learning process, and to transmit a healthy attitude toward making mistakes. The song and activity for introducing this lesson is taught in the first few weeks of school. Basically, the teacher is modeling a matter-of-fact tone and manner when relating real mistakes he or she has made and how they were "fixed" or what was "learned." Humor and humility are essential for this exercise. The mistakes shared must be true in order to lend authenticity. A note of drama also appeals to the children's interest in real life anecdotes and guarantees their attention.

The Mistakes Lesson

1. Gather the children for singing. Introduce the song, "It's OK to Make Mistakes" (see Table 2-2).

2. The song is included after the sharing by the teacher and then the children are invited to share a time when they made a mistake. Example: "One day I was carrying too many cups of water, and I spilled them all in the hallway. I fixed my mistake by getting a mop and cleaning up the mess." Sing refrain.

3. Invite several children in a row to share a mistake and how they fixed it or what they learned. Sing refrain again after they have shared.

Songs

During the beginning of the year there are two songs that are taught, which help to make everyone more comfortable about sharing their emotions and sharing mistakes. Even if you don't have a gift for singing, these basic chants are easy for anyone to use. They readily engage your students as you begin to lay the groundwork for emotional literacy in your classroom.

The age range for the songs is 5 to 9 years old. Songs are not necessary for 10 through 12 year olds.

Once you have their attention in this way, you can quickly intersperse your own "short anecdotal story" regarding a feeling, need, or mistake, and then illicit some of their own examples. They are extremely eager to participate once you have shared your first authentic story. Then you can immediately go back to your "lesson" through the refrain of the song. This will keep things lively and engaging for quite a while, which will provide ample time for covering more territory each time you repeat the lesson.

The first song which is sung on the first or second day of school is called "The Feelings Song." The purpose is to teach a few feelings words and to give an example of when you, the teacher felt that feeling. Once that is done for the particular emotion, the teacher asks if anyone else has ever felt the same. Invariably, many hands shoot up, eager for a chance to share their examples. This activity teaches emotional vocabulary in a fun way, but it also gets across the commonality of uncomfortable feelings and can foster increased empathy.

The second song is called "It's OK to Make Mistakes." Again, the teacher introduces the song by sharing a time when he or she made a particular mistake. The teacher then shares how he or she fixed the mistake or if it couldn't be fixed, what was learned by making the mistake. The song is sung after the sharing, and then the children are invited to share a time when they made a mistake.

Table 2-1: Feelings Song

"It's ok to feel_______________, it's ok to feel _______________, it's ok to feel _________________. It's just a feeling that you have."

(Teacher verbalizes a time when he or she felt a particular emotion and asks if anyone else has felt that way. Allow time for a few students to share a time when they felt the same emotion. Then move on to the next emotion example. Feelings are divided into "Comfortable" or "Uncomfortable" categories and named as such by the teacher. For example, "first I'll tell you about an uncomfortable feeling I had the other day, "I was feeling nervous because I had to sing in front of the class." Then sing the song and insert "nervous".)

Then after completing the group of emotions and child examples for that day, add the ending to the song, which is:

"It's ok to feel_______________, it's ok to feel _______________, it's ok to feel _________________. It's just a feeling that you have."
"It's safe to let your feelings show, feel each one, then let it go."

Table 2-2: Mistakes Song

The same tune can be used for the Mistakes Song.

"It's ok to make mistakes, it's ok to make mistakes, it's ok to make mistakes. They help us while we're learning."

The teacher inserts a mistake he or she has made and tells how it was fixed or what was learned. "One day I was trying to carry too many cups of water and I spilled them all in the hallway. I fixed my mistake by getting the mop and cleaning up my mess."

Sing the refrain again. Then the children are invited to share a mistake they have made and how they fixed it or what they learned. Continue singing the song in between each example. For each new round, the teacher can share first in order to make it safer for students to share.

Source: Tulum Dothe, 1987

Musical Notes for the Feelings Song and the Mistakes Song

It's ok to feel ____________________________________

C EG G A G (or GG if more than one syllable)

(Repeat above three times)

It's just a feeling that you have!

A A A C D D C

Share feelings and examples (just talking)

It's safe to let your feelings show

A A A G C DD C

Feel each one then let it go!

A A G C D D C

Language and Tone

It is critical to instill careful attention to language and tone of voice at the beginning of the year.

The language atmosphere of the classroom should be as respectful as possible first so that there will be a safe climate for the vulnerability and self-honesty that the Gifts and Challenges lesson requires. The terminology used with the children comes from the book, *Compassionate Classroom.* In this model, there are two ways of speaking. One way is called "Giraffe" language, which is gentle, respectful, and kind. The other way is called "Jackal" language, which is harsh, disrespectful, and unkind.

The teacher can model how those voices sound, using typical classroom examples. This always brings forth knowing looks and understanding from the children. Make a point at that time of stating how difficult it would be if children were to start scolding each other for using Jackal Language. Instead, suggest it would be more respectful to say kindly that we are trying to use Giraffe language. Use a small replica of a giraffe or other symbol to inspire the students toward their goal to speak in that type of language. Remind children that they do not have to be perfect at this and that everyone is learning to improve together.

Giraffe Language is *gentle, respectful, and kind.* The giraffe reminds us of this because it has a large heart. Giraffes are also very tall so they can see many ways to meet needs. They can stick their long necks out to say the truth about their own feelings and to care about others.

Jackal Language is *harsh, disrespectful, and unkind.* The jackal reminds us of this because it is low to the ground and is ready to attack. The jackal can only see what it needs. They don't know how to say the truth of what they are feeling or to show caring for others.

From *Compassionate Classroom, pg. 71-73*

The Peace Corner

The Peace Corner is central to the classroom. Providing this space shows the children that these ideas have real value and an important place in our world.

The Peace Corner is set up as a beautiful and calm haven where children can go when they want to slow down and feel their emotions, calm down after an upset, or choose to explore a selection of peaceful activities displayed on the peace shelf.

The Feelings Wheel and Needs Wheel reside there, as well as the form used by the Peacemaker to facilitate a conflict resolution or "problem solving." The wheels are available for children to look at and small gems can be used for children to mark their own feelings or needs on a particular day. In addition, there is a set of needs cards and feelings cards for sorting, which are based on the wheels.

Our Peace Corner also includes books on feelings and a collection of stories about inspiring leaders and peacemakers. There are many soothing activities such as a sand tray with stones, a small collection of glass gems or rocks to touch and admire, beautiful nature pictures, and a Buddha board for painting water designs.

Other activities include a yoga mat and cards for exercising quietly outside. Tags for walking on the labyrinth or taking a short walk in the garden can be used with the teacher's permission.

To ensure respectful use of the Peace Corner, we use a timer so children don't monopolize the area or misuse their work time by over staying. It also protects the individual child from being hurried by other students who are eager to use the space. We are fostering a meaningful experience with these materials, so 10 to 15 minutes feels reasonable and respectful. This allows children some genuinely private and peaceful moments, while teaching the value of quiet alone time.

The Peacemaker

The class peacemaker role is modeled and taught at the beginning of each year. A student is given the job of helping to solve problems between individual students and of facilitating the weekly peace circle. The role of peacemaker can be assigned monthly or bi-weekly, according to the make-up of the class. The child who is taking on this role needs to have at least two weeks of doing this job to really absorb the problem-solving procedure and become effective as a facilitator.

A mock problem solving is done by the teacher for the whole class at the beginning of each year. This illustrates the steps and highlights the non-threatening nature of the process. It can be repeated occasionally throughout the year as a refresher.

Initially, the teacher sits in on a real problem-solving situation to support each child who is learning the role of peacemaker. After a time, most children can lead this process on their own, but exercise caution when there are larger groups or argumentative children who need to problem solve.

Designate a small space on the board for problems set up with five numbered spaces for problems needing to be solved. A brief cooling off period is required before children put problems on the board. Many issues can be solved to children's satisfaction by using a simple "I Message" (see Table 2-4). This technique also prevents the peacemaking process from being over-used. Teachers may talk to their class about this and provide a second area for "I Messages" or just inquire regarding each problem- "Do you think this problem can be solved with an "I Message"?"

Problems are addressed at least once a week. The peacemaker takes the problems in order when possible. The peacemaker can usually handle two or three "simple" problems (involving only two children) in a session lasting a total of 20 minutes. (If a more complicated problem takes that long, just do one problem for that day.) This seems to be a comfortable amount of time for both the student peacemaker and the teacher.

The point is for the problem solving to happen frequently enough to give the children confidence in the process. If there is too long of a wait to solve the problems, the children will lose faith in the process and there will be emotional unrest in the classroom and on the playground.

Table 2-3: Peacemaking Guidelines

Peacemaking

1. Are you each willing to solve the problem?

2. Are you each willing to listen without interrupting?

3. Are you each willing to be as honest as you can?

4. Who is asking for this problem to be solved?

5. ______________________, would you like to use the Feelings Wheel and give an "I Message"? (Ask each child the same question.)

6. ________________________, does the problem feel solved to you? (Ask each child the same question.)

If anyone feels the problem is not solved, continue with 9, 10, 11, & 12 then back to 8.)

7. ____________________, would you like to use the Needs Wheel and identify the needs you were trying to meet? (Once the students all take a turn, the teacher or peacemaker can briefly point out needs that are the same.)

8. (Ask the child who requested the problem-solving) __________________, would you like to shake hands on it, give a hug, or just smile and say "thank you for listening"?

9. Does anyone have anything more to say that would help us solve the problem?

10. Can anyone think of what could be done differently next time to avoid the problem?

11. Do you each feel the problem is solved now?

12. ______________________, would you like to use the Needs Wheel and identify the needs you were trying to meet? (Teacher or peacemaker points out needs that are the same.) Then go back to number 8.

Once the problem is solved, go to the teacher and make sure it is a good time to announce that "The problem between ___________________ and _____________ has been solved." The rest of the class claps when the announcement has been made. The peacemaker then erases the names from the problem solving list.

The Peace Circle

At our Peace Circle each week, we think of four places in the world to send our peaceful thoughts. The peacemaker has the special privilege of presenting the peace candle and arranging the smaller candles (four tea candles with batteries), along with written labels which remind us of where we are sending our peaceful thoughts. We light the central candle and sing one of the peace songs while circling the peace candle. "Imagine" by John Lennon is our favorite. Four children place the smaller candles throughout the room. Then the peacemaker snuffs out the main peace candle, saying "May Peace Prevail on Earth." The class repeats this sentence thoughtfully and respectfully. Next, the peacemaker reads an inspirational quote that the children discuss. Alternatively, a Virtues card is read from the children's deck compiled by the Virtues Project International.

Inspirational Quotes

The idea for the "inspirational quotes" part of the Peace Circle came about in an unusual manner. What follows is how we first discovered that we had this need.

Every Wednesday, right after music class we would sometimes do an extra song or game. On that particular day the children who were our usual enthusiastic song-leaders just seemed listless and not at all in the mood. Noticing that the somber note seemed to be a prevailing one, we stopped the activity and went around the circle, asking each child to share if something was bothering him or her. This was shortly after 9-11 and so as we went around the circle some children mentioned they were worried about that, others said they were fighting with their brothers or sisters, or that a pet had died. In general, there was just a lot of sadness floating around circle that day. So we talked about how it was natural to feel that way and good to honor those feelings, but that we didn't want to get stuck there for a long time. Somehow, the idea that getting inspired by quotes or songs could help to cheer us up was mentioned in the conversation. We then listened to a short poem from Mattie Stepanik's book called *Just Peace: A Message of Hope*. The mood lifted, and we went on with our day.

A few days later, one of our older students came to class excited about what she had to share. Coincidentally, she had noticed that there were inspiring quotes printed on the back of a box of sandwich bags! So linking this to our previous conversation, while riding to school that morning, she took it upon herself to copy them down for us. We immediately decided to read one. We discussed its meaning, and then dumped the rest into a beautiful bowl and placed it in a central position on our

Circle table. Later, after searching some books for simple quotes that the students would understand, we added those to the "sandwich bag" collection. From that day forward, each Wednesday, after we sang a peace song, our Peacemaker read one inspirational quote aloud to the class. Children would then comment on the meaning of the quote. They often used their own personal anecdotes to illustrate their point. These thoughts could be quite deep, endearingly humorous, sometimes a little confused, but always touchingly earnest.

In recent years, the children have begun helping to create our own inspirational quotes. A topic is suggested such as kindness, friendship, or patience. The children then brainstorm possible quotes which are written on the board. Then a few ideas are selected and combined into one sensible and catchy line. Sometimes the individual ideas are brilliant just as they are. We have added these to our existing collection of quotes. We also write one on the board, which remains there for several days so that we can refer to it as needed. The children also have any of these quotes to choose from when they fill out a section on "Inspirational Thoughts" in their Gifts and Challenges Journal.

The original quote that we read during one brainstorming session was "You can't succeed if you don't get out there and try." The discussion of the meaning of this generated ideas and quotes of their own. Here are a few.

"You have to have courage to try something new."

"You can keep trying and maybe you will make a basket."

"You should never give up on yourself."

"You have to try something new and have courage or you won't be able to follow your dream."

Another day we talked about the meaning of Patience. The following quotes came from that talk.

"Patience is Peace."

"Patience is the key to happiness."

"The more patient you are, the more good natured you'll be in the future."

"The more patient you are, the better person you'll be."

"Patience means waiting in peace."

"Patience is good for you."

"Patience is the best thing you can have."

In another session we talked about Kindness and Respect.

"Someone who seems different may have amazing ideas."

"Respect nature and plants as you would humans."

"Kindness is when you care for family and friends and when you respect people around you and keep nice feelings flowing around the room."

"Kindness is a very strong feeling. Being kind is respecting other's feelings and standing up for your friends. It is also doing kind acts, supporting others when they are facing challenges, and speaking in gentle (giraffe) language. You can do a kind act by helping a teacher, parent, or anyone."

Some of the great rewards in having the children discuss quotes and generate their own are that it helps illustrate the commonality of human experience, while bringing empathy and compassion into awareness. It shows children their own wisdom as they seek to understand and discuss the meaning and the message inside the quote. They become increasingly articulate as they express their feelings and develop a deeper understanding of what goes wrong in problem situations that occur among classmates. Giving children time to hear and consider these bigger ideas regarding virtues and values sheds light on what it means to live in cooperation and respect as part of the human family.

Class Meetings

Weekly Class Meetings provide another format for addressing feelings as well as teaching the skill of giving sincere compliments. The concept of "I Messages" is taught as a way of expressing a concern in a kind and firm manner.

Table 2-4: How to Give an "I Message"

To introduce this technique, role-play the method for "I Messages" by using a made-up problem for your first example. State that "I Messages" are for telling another person your feelings about a problem using kindness, honesty, and power.

My common example is that I have a problem with another child taking too long on the swings.

1. I deliver it this way: (name of child)____________________________, I feel___________________ when you take so long on the swings and don't let me take a turn. In the future, I would like you to use the swing for a shorter time and let me have a turn, too.
2. The other child then respectfully says "I hear you."
3. Then the rest of the class claps because it takes courage to give an "I Message" and courage to receive one.

Be sure to stress eye contact from both parties as well as a respectful non-accusing tone of voice. The use of "you never" or "you always" can be illustrated. Point out that starting an "I Message" with the words "you always" or "you never" are examples of being accusing or jackal-like in tone. Discuss listening respectfully without making faces or interrupting to tell your own side. You can model incorrect ways of speaking and acting—pointing a finger, using a harsh tone of voice, or pouting. Showing the negative in an extreme way can help bring out the humor and highlight the pitfalls of what we don't want to happen.

When "I Messages" are done at class meetings we usually ask if there is anyone who would like to give an "I Message" and limit the number to five. That way we eliminate retaliating or too much negative content in each meeting. Dialogue regarding "I Messages" given at class meetings isn't practiced in our way of managing the meeting time.

"I Messages" can also be given at the request of a child during worktime or playtime. These are done in the presence of a teacher. This keeps the process safe so that a counter message is not given immediately after the first message. There is no interrupting allowed as the message is given. After the "I Message" is delivered and the receiver says respectfully, "I hear you", the teacher may want to ask, "Is there anything more to say that can help us understand the problem?" This allows the receiver fair treatment in case the issue is a little deeper. Finally, end the interchange with "Do you both feel happy and understood? Do you feel respected and that you can trust each other?" If both parties are not satisfied, you can invite them to write their names in the problem solving box.

We also ask for five compliments during the same meeting. It is effective for the teacher to model giving a few compliments at each meeting to ensure that everyone receives a well formulated compliment such as, "I would like to compliment you on your beautiful drawing. The colors you used are so bright and you take your time with each stroke you make," versus the common stand-bys, "You're a fast runner and a good friend."

Table 2-5: Compliment Procedure

1. Child sits in front of another child who is to be complimented.
2. Try to give examples for each thing you are complimenting. _______________, I would like to compliment you on your friendliness—you always remember to include others in your games, your gift for reading—you have such good expression, and your talent for jump roping—you got to a really high number last time.
3. Both children make eye contact with one another.
4. The complimenter must have a compliment in mind before sitting down. (It is hard to be waiting for a compliment or have the person forget what they were going to say.)
5. The person receiving the compliment also makes eye contact and says thank you.

Put Downs

Finally, we introduce the idea of put downs—what they are, why children might be doing this behavior, and a procedure for handling it on the day the put down was received. The idea is to empower the children to recognize a put down, assertively stand up for themselves by naming it, and to ask for assistance from a teacher (this is not tattling). The child who has given the put down owes the other child a card and a compliment before the end of the day. This is done in the presence of a teacher to ensure respect and receptivity on both sides. The child who has given the put down often needs prior help to form the compliment as an antidote for the put down versus an unrelated compliment. The card is a beautifully drawn picture presented as a gesture of goodwill toward the offended student.

Table 2-6: How to Demonstrate Handling a Put Down

At the beginning of the year, read a book that illustrates insults, put downs and teasing. Preferably, choose one which talks about the motivations behind put downs or verbal bullying. Then, (as a teacher playing the role of a child), act out a mild put down scenario (with another child or teacher assistant) who is either giving or receiving a put down. Following the scene, get input from the class regarding how the child might feel on receiving the put down. Then, explain that whenever you feel you have received a put down, you may: 1. Ask a teacher for help in giving an "I Message." 2. "I Message" is given. For example: "_________________ when you said that I wasn't good at soccer, I felt______________________. In the future please don't comment on my soccer playing." 3. The child receiving the "I Message" gives respectful eye contact and says "I hear you." 4. Following that, the child who has given the put down owes the first child a card (nice picture) and a compliment related to the area in which the put down was given. (The teacher is present during this interchange.) Prior to giving the compliment, the child is coached by the teacher to make sure that the compliment is in the appropriate area and that this child is spoken to with gentleness and encouragement to make things "right" with the classmate.

Ways for Solving Problems

The primary methods provided for children to bring up problems are:

1. Using the problem solving box on the whiteboard (addressed weekly by a child peacemaker along with teacher support).
2. Making an on-the-spot verbal request for teacher support in giving an "I Message" to another child.
3. Writing a problem in the class meeting agenda folder.
4. There is also the technique of using a hand signal if a student is not respecting another student's body or if there is need of an immediate teacher response.

There is another method for addressing problems that a child believes cannot wait for a day or two. It is called the Problem Box, which consists of a see-through box alongside a small basket of colored paper tickets. This is placed on a table or shelf in plain view. The children can just take a colored ticket and write their name or initials and place it in the box. Children are free to remind you that the ticket is there. The teacher or assistant can then take the child aside and find out the nature of the problem before the child goes home. This technique is very helpful because if the child just needs redirecting to a more typical method of problem solving, reassurance that things can be worked out on the following day, or a mini problem solving or "I Message" with teacher guidance at that moment, it will often avoid an upset at home and unnecessary parental worry over minor problems.

Children can be taught the proper timing and use of each of these methods during the introduction of classroom ground rules.

All of these techniques for creating a peaceful and emotionally safe classroom have evolved organically and worked well in my classroom for many years. **However, be sure to consistently showcase and advertise to the whole class all the options for addressing problems. If this is neglected, those shyer or unaware children who need these experiences won't make full use of them. Parents can sometimes express concern about unkind comments, teasing, or bullying and then want immediate "action." Redirecting this concern toward encouraging their child to make use of the problem solving techniques already set in place, will keep the process safe and empower each student. To prevent misunderstandings, educating the parents thoroughly about your own classroom procedures for handling put downs and teasing should be a top priority at the beginning of the year.**

Section 3: The Lesson

Gifts and Challenges Story

"When you are born, you have certain gifts, things that will be very easy for you, fun, and don't take lots of practice, and that you just love to do. These gifts are yours to use and to share. At the same time, you have certain challenges, things you need to practice, that take more trying, that sometimes you don't like to do at all because you don't know how or you think you can't. These challenges are yours to practice and make better. Everyone has both gifts and challenges.

THERE IS NO ONE WHO HAS ALL GIFTS AND NO CHALLENGES.

THERE IS NO ONE WHO HAS ALL CHALLENGES AND NO GIFTS.

Everyone is special and unique. That is what makes everyone valuable and equally important. Sometimes you know your gifts and challenges, and sometimes you don't. You can't give your gifts away to someone else and you can't make your challenges go away just by wishing.

You have choices about what you do with your gifts. If you have a certain gift you could use it and enjoy it, you could share it with someone else, you could forget about it and never use it, or you could use your gift to make another person feel bad. Even if you weren't born with a particular gift, you can still practice that thing until it gets much easier and becomes a talent—something you're very good at.

You also have choices about what you do with your challenges. If you have a certain challenge, you can practice it until it gets much easier, or it can stay a bit of a challenge but slowly get better and better if you practice enough. You could have a challenge and show others how you got better at it, you could have a challenge and just give up, or you could have a challenge and use it to make yourself feel bad or try to get sympathy from others.

My job as your teacher is to help you discover your gifts and use them, and it's also to help you discover your challenges and show you ways to practice them. The way that I do that is to look for work on the shelves that will match your gifts, and help you to use them well. I also look for work that will go with your challenges and that will help you to get better at them. Many of you are often good at finding your own work that matches what you need, especially when you know what you love to do and also when you know what you need to practice. So, you don't need my help too often. Does every person in our class need the same work, the same book, or the same math and reading at the same time? Does it make sense for me to keep on teaching the alphabet to ___________ when she already knows the sounds? Does it make sense for me to make __________ practice kicking a soccer ball when he already knows how to do that? Does it make sense for me to teach ___________ division before he knows addition well? Should I tell __________ to wait until everybody catches up to her, before she uses her gift for math? No!

Everybody works at their own special speed, in their own special time, for their own special reasons. How do you think you would feel if I asked you not to use your gift because it might make somebody feel bad? Or what if I asked you to wait until everybody got as good as you are at your gift before you could use it again? How do you think you would feel if I told you that you shouldn't have your challenges, and that you should already know how to do everything and that you'd better hurry up?

When you see someone using their gift, you have choices about how you might feel. You might choose to feel admiration, be happy for the person, or inspired. These are positive feelings. You could also choose to feel sad, jealous, or less important. These are negative feelings.

When you see someone practicing their challenge you have choices about how you might feel. You might feel admiring of their determination, inspired, or proud of their efforts. These are positive. You might feel sad for them, better than they are, or contemptuous. These are negative. You also have choices about what you say or do. In both cases you can choose to be encouraging or discouraging. Encouraging words are: "Your work is beautiful." "You really enjoy that." "It's fun to watch you do that work so well." "Congratulations…" Discouraging words are: "That looks terrible." "That doesn't look like a ______." "Why is that taking you so long?" "Oh, that work is so easy—you're still doing it?!"

Because we want our classroom to be a safe place to learn for EVERYONE, what we are trying to learn is to use encouraging words with each other. Let's think of some things we could say to someone who is practicing their gift…their challenge…Now I want you to see what my own gifts and challenges are. I've written as many as I could think of on the board, and I'll put a G next to each gift and a C next to each challenge."

Preparation for Gifts and Challenges Lesson

[The Gifts and Challenges lesson needs a morning or an entire day for full exploration. The following is helpful in setting up the best "first" experience for your class.]

1. Prime students for full attendance. Talk about it at Circle, but don't tell too much—keep the element of surprise as part of the enticement.

2. Prepare a letter to send home to parents that states what is being done and why full attendance is important.

3. Make copies of Gifts and Challenges charts for students to fill out.

4. Once the charts are filled out by the students, they can be copied so parents have a duplicate for reference during at-home conversations. Make extra copies in case parents want to fill out and share with their children.

5. Have materials for art activities, music, outdoor activities, or other choices that are not typically set up for everyday use.

6. Have staff or helpers prepared to go outside to supervise those whose gifts need to be done outdoors.

7. Plan for a follow-up Circle with each child sharing a gift that he or she practiced.

Facilitating the Gifts Day

1. **Tell the story.** When the children come together for the first Gifts and Challenges day of the year, excitement can already be in the air and circulating throughout the classroom before any words are spoken because of the older students' prior experience. But if this is the first time for you and your students or if you don't have a multi-age classroom, you can still make use of a sense of mystery and drama as you launch into telling your version of the "story" of the basic gifts and challenges idea. Keep your examples real and call on your oral story telling skills. The children are usually mesmerized by hearing about something that actually happened to someone just like them. The other option is to tell the version that begins this chapter, which is a bit longer. Choose what you think will resonate with your particular students for the initial lesson. You can always go back to add more information for discussion on subsequent days if needed.

Short version of the story

One day a long time ago, there was a boy in my class named Anthony. He was trying to do his homework one night, and he began to cry. His mom called me and told me all about it. Earlier that day another child had walked by as he was doing his reading workbook, saying "What!" "You're only in Book 1?" "You should be in Book 2 by now!" Anthony was so discouraged by the time he got home that he felt he couldn't do anything at all. So I talked with Anthony for a while and reminded him of all his talents in art, in soccer, and music. I told him that he was in just the right reading book for what he was trying to learn. After that, he became calm and went back to his work feeling better. When this happened it made me think there might be a way to teach all the children about how it's fine to be good at some things and have trouble with other things. Then it happened- the idea for Gifts and Challenges popped into my mind. We tried the lesson the next day. The children understood it and loved doing the first Gifts and Challenge Day. So now, every year each class has a lesson on Gifts and Challenges.

2. **Demonstrate how to fill out the charts.** Once you have told the story, you can begin the demonstration by filling out your own chart via large whiteboards made up to list each category. To help keep their eyes on just one category at a time, the other charts face the wall until you are about to fill them out. Remember to be anecdotal and light in your tone, as well as totally honest about your own gifts and challenges. Don't take too long in doing this, especially if another teacher or assistant is also going to share in the demonstration. If the attention span is waning, have the other adult fill out only one category while the children are watching, and then complete the rest at a later point in the morning.

   "Now I want you to see what my own gifts and challenges are. I'll put a G next to my gifts and a C next to my challenges." "Starting with the Thinking area, hmmm, Reading—that's a gift. I love to read about history." "Talking—that's a challenge if I have to give a speech." There is no need to comment on each one, but include enough to keep it interesting and authentic. Some items might be both a gift and a challenge so record it as G/C. If the subject has never been tried, use I for "interested."

3. **Involve the children in filling out their own charts.** Once you have passed out the charts, you can divide the group into those who are independent and those who will need assistance. As the children begin filling out their own charts, you can sit with the youngest group or those who may be non-readers and take them through the charts all at once. Older students can go off and fill out their charts independently or in small groups. They are usually quite honest about how they see themselves in terms of their gifts and challenges. Surprisingly, they do not influence each other as they do their own charts. If that were to begin happening, separate the children involved and give a private talk to each about wanting to make sure that he or she is honest when filling out the charts. Emphasize that the charts are meant to help us see where we are in each area and that there are no right or wrong ways to do that. Emphasize that it's important for each student to mark what he or she thinks are gifts and challenges and not think about comparing charts with others. It may be helpful to briefly explain some of the words in the People and Kindnesses categories as you do your demonstration. Even so, it may also be necessary to answer a few individual questions about some of these terms again as the children are filling out their own charts.

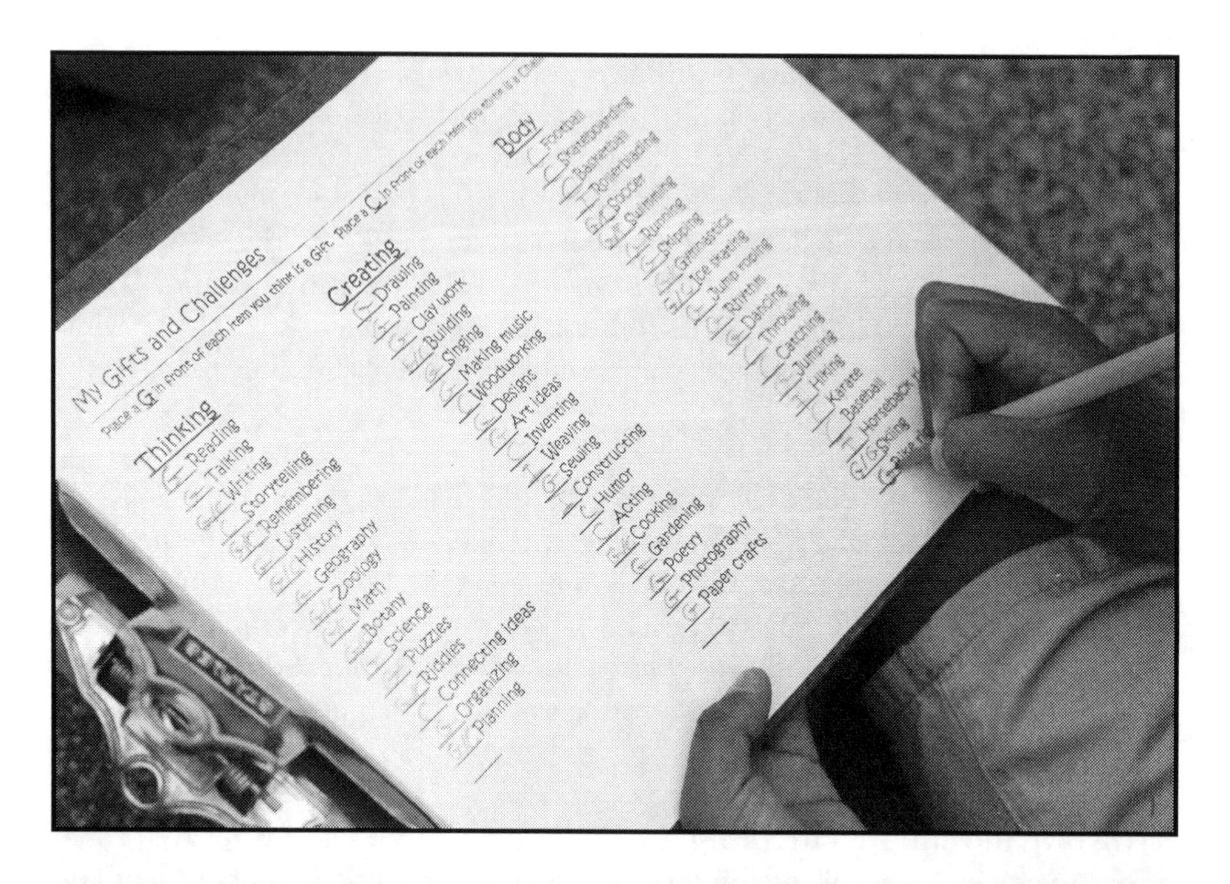
My Gifts and Challenges
Place a G in front of each item you think is a Gift.
Thinking
Reading
Talking
Writing
Storytelling
Remembering
Listening
History
Geography
Zoology
Math
Botany
Science
Puzzles
Riddles
Connecting ideas
Organizing
Planning
Creating
Drawing
Painting
Clay work
Building
Singing
Making music
Woodworking
Designs
Art ideas
Inventing
Weaving
Sewing
Constructing
Humor
Acting
Cooking
Gardening
Poetry
Photography
Paper crafts
Body
Football
Skateboarding
Basketball
Rollerblading
Soccer
Swimming
Running
Skipping
Gymnastics
Ice skating
Jump roping
Rhythm
Dancing
Throwing
Catching
Jumping
Hiking
Karate
Baseball
Skiing

4. **Transition to the exercising of gifts.** Children will finish at different times, so enlist those who are finished to help those who still need help (younger students, emerging readers). As more children have completed their charts, gather them in a small circle and quickly ask each child to tell one of their gifts and one of their challenges. This is quite engaging for them, since the experience of actually naming it out loud seems to be very empowering and energizing. Once they do that, they can choose a gift that they would like to do. Some like to carry their charts around with them so they can refer to possible choices for their gifts.

5. **Introduce the materials that are available.** The materials should be set up ahead of time in areas or centers of activity. Whatever you decide to give the children access to will color the experience of the day. All the usual classroom materials are available for use. Additional art, music, science, nature, and physical activities can also be offered. On our first try at this, we put out a table of clay; another with wire, spools, corks and so on for inventing; a painting table; and an area for sewing. We also set up wood construction with glue on a picnic table outside the classroom. There were seeds and small pots for planting in the gardening area, balls and jump ropes were a choice, as well as sidewalk chalking. These activities need not all be available on one day. Be judicious in the amount you offer, but not too sparse or there won't be a wide enough range or enough newness to generate excitement.

6. **Observe and guide sustained activity with a calm presence.** Be prepared for the excited noise, rapid motion, and general shuffling of many bodies during the decision making, material arranging, and social grouping that will accompany the starting point. This will abate and settle into a normal hum after about 10 to 15 minutes. If for some reason it remains chaotic for too long, regroup and settle on ground rules that will enable a worthwhile experience. If the children are young (6 to 9 years), it's possible, when they are set free to do their gifts, they might only follow what their friends want to do instead of truly looking at their own charts and choosing a gift to exercise. Reminders and suggestions can be given about this, but not too much intervention. It is important to respect the instinct to work in groups during the ages of 6 to 9 years old. It is equally important to remember that the teacher's role during this experience is as an observer and a ready admirer when engagement is sought by the students. A respectful "hands-off" attitude is the order of the day.

   As the initial chaos and noise settled down, we watched the concentration and joy take hold. Some children stayed with their first choice for a very long time, others jumped from activity to activity until they found their niche. I began to step into the outdoor games after about 30 minutes and suggest that these children choose another gift to exercise, not wanting Gifts day to become equated with playtime in their minds. There was initial resistance, but when they realized that there were many other interesting options, their joyful engagement returned. The occasional lone child did take up reading a book in the library or doing a series of math problems for quite a long time. I did intervene with these children eventually, so that they would have a chance to do at least one other gift before the morning ended.

7. **Allow uninterrupted time for full exploration.** When we did this the first day, we started around 9:00 or 9:15 a.m., and then we set the children free to do the actual activities by 10:00 a.m., since it took a while for the story and filling out of charts by the teachers and students. As a result, by 11:45 a.m., we had to stop for lunchtime. It was obvious at that time that many children were still in the middle of things and that good concentration and sustained attention for this activity could fill the afternoon as well. From this observation of their hunger for more of this "gifts day," came the reminder that children absolutely thrive on the uninterrupted time needed to complete a cycle of deep interest. So we extended the experience into the afternoon, which made us all happy. That day we worked up until the last possible moment, but on subsequent "gift days" we stopped a little early to share or talk about our experiences at Circle.

On one particular "gifts day" a child who loved to work with clay had spent the entire morning making wonderful tiny detailed figurines. When the bell rang for lunch, he looked up at me and said most earnestly while nodding his head, "We are doing this in the afternoon too, aren't we? "Of course, the answer had to be yes. Later that day, he was able to exercise his gift for gardening as he slowly and carefully placed seeds in a little pot, while gently telling other students how to position their seeds and the right amount of water to add. He went home that day with a deep sense of satisfaction and joy at what he was able to do with his time.

8. **Allow time for clean-up and sharing.** The room can look like a disaster with so many activities, but if a system is in place for clean-up and involves everyone equitably, it can be put back together quite quickly. Begin handing out jobs once everyone has been gathered back together at Circle. From that moment of calm, it is easier to give the job assignments clearly. Be sure to involve the children versus having the adults clean up, otherwise next time the teachers may see it as all too much trouble. As children finish jobs at different times, read to those students who are finished, and then once everyone has arrived, have them share verbally regarding their experience of the day. Possibly wait until the next morning to show any art projects or other tangible results of exercising the students' gifts. Another possibility is that the students could make an entry in their Gifts and Challenges Journal (see Section 9: The Journals) once they have finished cleaning up and save the verbal sharing for Circle the next day or at another convenient time on the same day.

Gifts and Challenges Circle

Following are some ideas for the content of a Circle related to Gifts and Challenges. Doing a feelings check-in by starting with the Feelings Song, is a lively and engaging way to begin a non-threatening discussion of feelings related to either Gifts or Challenges. Pick just one of these suggestions for enough content for a Circle time, plus read an inspirational quote to complete the time together. An additional caution regarding talking too much about the concepts vs. actually doing the activities: over-talking may have the unwanted result of shutting down enthusiasm and making it about a teacher lecture. Instead, the ideas will be more alive and long lasting if they are something that the children discover through experiencing a Gifts or Challenges day, being an actor in a role playing, or taking on the job of a challenge buddy.

Suggestions for Circle

1. **Rights to Emotional Safety**—Read aloud (from their own Gifts and Challenges Journal), or have children take turns reading rights, and include a short explanation or anecdote by the teacher or comments volunteered by the children.

2. **Each child sharing 1 gift, 1 challenge (aloud or on paper)**—Children can simply name a gift and a challenge by stating which category each is from and whether it's a gift or challenge.

3. **Setting a goal for 1 gift, 1 challenge for the day/week**—Children can write down which gift they will exercise and which challenge they will practice for the day/week.

4. **Check In**—What would you like to remember to do, regarding gift, challenge? What materials do you need? When will you do it? Do you need a challenge buddy? Would you like to share your gift?

5. **Use the Journal page for planning**—Use it for a gift or challenge. Remove the form and attach to the work plan.

6. **Challenge Buddy**—If applicable, set up challenge buddies for the day.

7. **Feelings Check In**—Go around the circle and ask who would like to share how they felt when they were exercising a particular gift.

The Importance of Acknowledging Gifts

Teachers need to know how to fully acknowledge their own and other's gifts.

To teach oneself and our students how to be thrilled by another's abilities and accomplishments is a worthy and challenging endeavor. The idea is to be in admiration and support of others on their personal learning journey, while giving that same attention and consideration to ourselves. Underlying this task is the unspoken fear that we are not enough as we are and that others are "more" in some unapproachable way. Hopefully, this work will shed light on the real truth of who we all are as humans—which is unique, valuable, and essential.

Emotional largesse comes out of natural confidence. This confidence comes from the deep understanding of one's own innate "all-rightness" wherever one is in the learning process.

As the children begin to discover what their own personal gifts and challenges are, they are given a more realistic view of themselves. This balanced perspective allows for the development of natural confidence and true humility versus the extremes of over-confidence or self-doubt. From this balanced place, children can see and delight in their own wonderful gifts as well as take pleasure in the shining abilities of others.

Practicing the language and art of acknowledgment is a crucial aspect of working with these ideas.

A full acknowledgment is accurate, truthful, sincere, and very specific. The receiver should feel the full attention and warmth of the acknowledger while the compliment is offered with enthusiastic conviction. Eye contact and tone of voice will deliver the sincerity of the message. The receiver will practice how to sit still for such pointed attention and to respond with a sincere thank you.

The practice of acknowledging children and adults can happen organically during the daily life of the classroom. It can also be modeled and carried out in the formal structure of class meetings, peace circles, or staff meetings. Over time, these understandings and abilities become more natural to everyone. They will also manifest in the growth of trust and respect among the adults. Most importantly, they will bear fruit in the sensitive comments which come through the children, as they show us their ability to understand and apply these truths to their lives.

For Further Class Discussion

The following aids can be used as a way to generate conversation at a group time, either preceding or following a Gifts and Challenges lesson. As you go through the lists, you can insert a time when you have experienced or felt the same, which will usually ignite eager participation by the students. Children can be coached to use these terms, as well as how to use an encouraging and sincere tone as they engage with their classmates. Teachers can model this with another teacher or child "actor" to help in establishing this practice. The lists can be introduced as guides to what we are acknowledging in someone's gift or supporting in someone's challenge.

Aids to Recognizing Gifts

- You are already very good at it.
- You get very happy while you are doing it. (You might start singing or humming as you do your gift.)
- You want to do it all the time, every chance you get.
- You get lots of ideas about it, often without even trying.
- You don't get discouraged. You stay determined even when it gets harder to do.
- You feel like jumping up and down when you've accomplished something in your gift area and you can't wait to share it with someone who cares.
- You're very curious about it—you want to know more and more about this topic.
- You admire this gift in someone else and you wish you knew how to do it. You ask lots of questions or you wonder about it often.

Qualities to acknowledge (admire) in someone's gift:

Ease
Care
Beauty
Concentration
Precision/Detail
Confidence
Accuracy
Grace

Aids to Recognizing Challenges

- You have tried to do it and you found it to be very hard.
- You might feel like crying when you can't do it or you are asked to do it.
- You try to avoid doing it.
- Whenever you think about it you feel confused and quickly try to think of something else.
- You don't want to try your challenge by yourself; you think it will be overwhelming.
- You are not interested when others talk about this topic or do this activity.
- You might feel sadness, envy, anger, or ashamed when you see someone else doing well in your challenge activity.

Qualities to acknowledge (admire) in someone while practicing their challenge

Courage
Determination
Humility
Effort
Risk taking
Stamina
Trust
Humor
Patience

Shedding Light on the Comparison Jungle

In most children there is a constant undercurrent, an inner dialogue of comparisons going on, which can be interrupted by giving children the opportunity to see themselves in a more balanced light. Recognizing our own gifts and accepting as natural, our own challenges, can serve to level this inner playing field in the mind of the child. The ease with which they welcome these ideas and articulately discuss them is a strong indication of the power of these simple concepts to positively influence the self-confidence of children.

Subsequent to the first presentation of the Gifts and Challenges lesson, ideally in the same week, it is very illuminating for the children if you and another adult enact a scene depicting the thought process that might go on in the mind of someone who is comparing their gift or challenge to someone else's gift.

The term "Comparison Jungle" was first used by an artist friend of mine, Randy Keeney. As she listened to me bemoan my inability to paint like another artist whose style I envied, she glibly said, "having fun in the Comparison Jungle?" For me, this was a breakthrough moment.

In considering the emotional harm children inadvertently cause themselves when looking at the differing abilities of their classmates; this Comparison Jungle idea came back to me. Hoping the children might respond to the concept and could be well served by this lesson in human nature, the Comparison Jungle role-play was presented. It proved to be an essential piece to the confidence building elements of the program and has worked extremely well for the students.

The lesson can take any form, but in our first demonstration, I tried to draw a simple flower while my "friend" was working on her own flower drawing. As I watched her work, I began to speak my own thoughts aloud, wishing I could draw just like my friend, wondering how she does it so well, returning to my own drawing with frustration and finally crumpling up my paper with great drama and tears.

A class discussion followed, in which the children were encouraged to share their observations about what I might have been doing to myself as I watched my friend exercise her gift. The comments they shared revealed a depth of understanding which was surprising. The children saw that I was getting in my own way by watching my friend too much. They pointed out that I was saying mean things to myself while I tried to draw. They suggested that I might ask my friend for some tips on how to draw a flower. In short, they got it! It was the perfect moment to introduce the term "Comparison Jungle" and give a simple definition.

You are in the "Comparison Jungle" when you are working on an activity or looking at your work and thinking that others are better and that you are worse. You have forgotten to concentrate and enjoy your own work.

As children work throughout the year, this idea is so helpful whenever they encounter any version of this difficulty in their own attitude toward their work or abilities. My students now use this term spontaneously in the classroom.

Gifts and Challenges Vocabulary–Children's Examples

There have been many examples of deep insight on the part of students while discussing their own abilities, admiring other's gifts, or in giving supportive advice to classmates or even teachers who may be facing difficulties.

For example, Julian (age 9), was commenting on a hypothetical example of someone comparing themselves to another. He said, *"She was caught between stress and accomplishment."* He further elaborated with confidence, *"I used to have a challenge for reading. Now it's one of my gifts."* He saw himself as so capable in an area that could have remained a source of poor self-image or shame.

Another young student commented on what to do when you are frustrated by a challenge while comparing yourself to someone who has a gift in that area. Rory, (age 8), said *"You could ask that student who has a gift with it to give you some tips about how to do it."* She later added, *"You can do another of your gifts to calm you down."* What a wise approach! How liberating to be unencumbered by the jealousy or self-doubt which can often accompany watching someone do something well that happens to be your challenge.

Ten year old Cole, while encouraging a teacher as she was facing a sports challenge, said, *"Now remember Amanda, it's a challenge for a reason and don't expect it to become a gift in a day."*

After Nicolai had finished playing his violin piece, Alex said, *"I think that music made the sun come out!"* One particularly insightful quote that the whole class came up with was, *"Rise to your challenges, don't fear them."*

Dari (age 9), said, *"Some people have a secret gift."*

All these comments came straight from the heart and were the result of being immersed in the on-going conversation about gifts and challenges that became an organic part of our regular school days.

Role Playing for Gifts and Challenges

After the initial presentation, it is important to give voice to children's internalized negative thoughts by demonstrating several other role-playing scenarios. This will highlight the fact that everyone has these kinds of thoughts at one time or another and that it is just human nature to have these tendencies. The essential thing is to be able to "catch yourself" when you are doing this kind of thinking and to make sure that everyone knows about this, so that we can help each other.

In my classroom, the most often used role-play is the aforementioned one on the Comparison Jungle.

All of the scripts have strong possibilities for empowering the children, so after the Comparison Jungle script, it does not matter which one comes next. The very idea of the universality of this type of thinking can be such a revelation for the children. As you watch them during one of these activities, you will be amazed to see the almost visible sigh of relief as this knowledge is collectively absorbed. Here is the list of role-plays which is accompanied by a brief script for each one.

- **Comparison Jungle Script**
- **Self Put Down Script**
- **Put Down Script**
- **One-Upmanship Script**
- **Being Frozen Script**

Comparison Jungle Script

Since this is the first Script tried with your children, it is safer and more effective to act this out with a co-worker instead of a child.

1. Coach the co-worker ahead of time regarding his or her part in the scene. Make suggestions for dilemmas and lines.

2. Teacher #1: Sitting on the floor trying to draw a______________, while Teacher #2 is sitting right beside completely absorbed in drawing a beautiful ______________.

3. Teacher #1 begins to think out loud in a very negative comparative manner. "I wish I could draw like_____________________. How does she do that? I just can't stand my drawing! I'll never get it to look right!" Teacher #1 starts to crumple paper, and gets very dramatic and frustrated.

4. At this point, involve the children in noticing what Teacher #1 is doing to make this problem worse—not concentrating on her own work, not being patient with herself, wishing to be like someone else, not saying encouraging things to herself, not asking for tips, not really trying in a calm and concentrating way. You can also draw ideas from children about what could have been done differently in the scene to stay out of the Comparison Jungle.

5. Reenact scene: This time the frustrated teacher remembers out loud that it takes practice to get good at drawing, that maybe she could ask the "expert" how she does it, that she could admire her friend's gift instead of making herself feel worse, or that she could think about one of her own gifts for comfort and then ask for help or suggestions from someone she trusts.

Self Put Down Script

Invite two or more children to help you act out this scene. Coach the "actors" ahead of time regarding their parts in the scene. Make suggestions for possible situation and props.

Scene: The put down child has tried to do a particular work and is having great difficulty with the task.

The put down child starts making negative comments about his or her abilities such as "I'm terrible at…""My writing, spelling …. is the worst in the world!" "I always make the same mistakes!" The second child or teacher walks by and gently says, "It sounds like you're really frustrated." The first child responds with, "I'm just no good at this!"

The second child or teacher says, "Giving self put downs really makes it worse, so please stop and take a moment to get calm and be kind to yourself by remembering that you are special and thinking about one of your own gifts."

The put down child reluctantly agrees. They do some breathing together. The helper tells a funny story, joke, or an amusing incident regarding the work.

The child or teacher reads **Encouraging Thoughts** from the put down child's journal. A child or teacher helps the child with a tip or encourages the child to try again with a more patient, hopeful attitude.

The self put down child models approaching a difficult task with positive talk, like:

"I know this is hard for me, but I think I can do it if I keep trying." and "I've been able to do hard things before. I just have to believe in myself." The self put down child models getting better at the task or going to ask for help in a way that is positive toward him or herself and the helper.

Put Down Script

Invite two or more children to help act out this scene or do it with an assistant.

1. Coach the "actors" ahead of time regarding their parts in the scene. Make suggestions for situation and lines.

2. The first child is doing his or her work. The second child comes along and says, "That's not a very good________________." (In a mean tone of voice.)

3. The child who receives the put down reacts with anger, sadness, defeat…

4. The first child thinks out loud, "I'm so much better at________________ than ____________________! I'm just the very best in the class!"

5. The first child goes on to give put downs to a few more children.

6. At this point, begin to ask the audience how the receivers might be feeling.

How does it feel to be in a class where this happens a lot?

What can the child do instead of believing the put down?

7. Guide children to the **Rights to Emotional Safety** list.

8. Go back to role play and show possible confident responses to a put down.

9. For example, to "That's not a very good________________," the child can say "I'm happy with my work," "Please don't talk about my work that way," "This is a work in progress, please respect my concentration," and so on.

One-Upmanship Script

Invite two or more children to help act out this scene or do it with an assistant.

1. Coach the "actors" ahead of time regarding their parts in the scene. Make suggestions for situation and lines.

2. Child #1 says, "Oh, I'm so happy, I just finished my addition facts!"

3. Child #2 says, "Oh, I finished those a long time ago!"

4. Give several examples of Child #2 engaging in one-upmanship. Then name it as that. "Child #2 is doing something. That "something" is called "one-upmanship"." Illicit from the children what exactly happens in that situation. Get input from the class on how they might respond to a classmate who is doing that.

5. Reenact the scene.

6. Child #1 says, "Oh, I'm so happy, I just finished my addition facts!"

7. Child #2 says, "Oh, I finished those a long time ago!"

8. Child # 1 says, "That's called "one-upmanship." "Please let me enjoy my accomplishments without comments about yours."

Or

9. Child #1 thinks out loud, "__________________ is in the Comparison Jungle and trying to make him or herself feel better by saying this. I won't let that comment upset me."

Or

10. Child # 2 says, "I'm sorry, it really does feel great when you finish a set of facts doesn't it!"

Being Frozen Script

Invite two or more children to help act out this scene.

1. Coach the "actors" ahead of time regarding their parts in the scene. Make suggestions for dilemmas and lines.

2. The frozen child—sitting in front of work, sighing, grimacing, head in hands, etc.

3. Another child walks by and says in a light, positive tone, "Oh, getting ready to do __________, huh?"

4. The frozen child moans dramatically!

5. The other child walks away towards his or her own work area.

6. The frozen child is also thinking out loud, "This work is impossible." "I don't know where to start." "I just can't do this." "My head hurts."

7. A second child or teacher walks by and says domething like "Hmmm, I thought _________ started that work a while ago and he or she is still just sitting there. I wonder what's going on."

8. The frozen child is still non-verbally struggling and looking more frantic.

9. The first child comes along again and sees distress and asks "______, are you frozen?" The frozen child answers in a loud voice, "YES!!" The first child asks, "Would you like some help?" The frozen child starts to cry or looks very overwhelmed.

10. The helper suggests spending some time in the peace corner or getting a drink or snack to break the "frozen spell" and then sets up a time to meet during that work period to give help.

The children often spontaneously add dramatic and humorous elements to the enactments, so use the above as a skeletal outline. Afterwards, get ideas from the group about how it looks and feels to be in any of these roles. This part is very important in order to highlight the universality of these situations.

Challenge Days

Challenge days are set apart as a distinct experience from the Gifts and Challenges Lesson. Once the class has experienced at least one or two Gifts days, they will be ready to approach the subject of Challenges. One of the most important parts of this Lesson is the role of the teacher who will be self-disclosing and highlighting one of his or her challenges. This is the first Challenge Day activity and must come before the children are set free to work on their own challenges.

For example, having named my challenge in cooking, another teacher volunteered to help me with my difficulty. We had prepared the materials for the demonstration in advance, but this was all a surprise to the children. The teacher who was to be my "challenge buddy" was well known by the children for her gift in cooking. This offered a great opportunity to have some fun by demonstrating typical human avoiding behaviors such as being obviously distracted, looking bored, needing a drink, making up excuses to go to another part of the room, making simple mistakes in learning, or even forgetting what was just said by the helping teacher! The aim is for a playful yet realistic drama which will engage the children, but not go too far into silliness or seriousness. The commonality of this lesson is to be showcased rather than overshadowed by the exuberance or personalities of the performers.

The attitude of both players in this scene is essential to effective modeling of a healthy and accepting attitude toward challenges. The elements of gentle humor and patience toward oneself are key lessons to instill in the children as they watch this demonstration unfold. Of course, the teacher doing the self-disclosing needs to really have a challenge in the area being shown or the authenticity of the lesson will be compromised and inevitably the children will sense this. The teacher who is helping also has a pivotal role in modeling trust by how caringly she demonstrates encouraging language, how she brings her friend's attention back, how she breaks down the task into easy steps, the tips she gives when mistakes are made, and the way she shows acceptance, patience, and confidence in her friend's ability to improve.

Qualities of a Challenge Buddy

A challenge buddy is a trusted guide, someone to have as your partner when facing one of your challenges. It can be lonely or scary to face a challenge alone, but somehow the task can seem lighter and more possible with the moral support of someone who is willing to stand by quietly, give encouragement, or offer tips for approaching the challenge. The children love to offer their help in this way, with wonderful experiences gained on both sides of the partnership.

Following is a general list regarding the qualities and the role of a challenge buddy. This can be discussed briefly before the children are paired up for a challenge day.

An alternative is to make it into a poster to be on hand during the activity or on a daily basis.

A Helpful Challenge Buddy

1. Speaks and acts gently toward the challenge partner.

2. Treats the challenge partner kindly.

3. Acts with patience.

4. Pays close attention to the partner the whole time.

5. Gives simple instructions for each step of the challenge.

6. Respects the feelings of the child being helped, asks permission before giving tips.

7. Makes encouraging comments like "you're getting better," "keep at it."

8. Stays with the partner until the child is ready to try the challenge alone.

9. Is willing to try different ideas if the first ones don't seem to help.

10. Congratulates or acknowledges the risk, improvement, or effort of the challenge partner.

Challenge Buddies—Young and Old

When pairing children up for the first Challenge Day, it is automatically organized around ability versus age. In matching children who had gifts in the challenge area of another, and soliciting volunteers to be challenge buddies, the process naturally yielded some unusual partnerships. So even though "age doesn't matter" is a lesson that we all want to "teach," having a six year old help a very adept eight year old reader work on her listening challenge says more than any words can convey. In this partnership, the ingenuity in forming the lesson and practice activity came directly from the younger student without any prompting from the teachers. The enthusiasm of the younger child, as well as the genuine humility and graciousness of the older student was unplanned and uncoached.

In the upper elementary level, the teacher set up the first Challenge Day partnerships between 6th graders and 4th graders. In one interchange a 4th grade boy was giving an older one tips on how to write a poem. He was very clear and very patient as the older student worked it out and read back his initial results. The comment was an upbeat, "now you're getting the hang of it." This type of spontaneous and kind encouragement was the rule rather than the exception in so many of the challenge buddy interactions.

However the couples match up, the quality of these days is one of kindness and empowerment.

Challenge Buddy Sequence

1. After the "teacher challenge" demonstration is over, a brief talk about the qualities of a trustworthy helper and the attitude of the one being "helped" is needed before proceeding to the activity for the children.

2. Some small posters which list the qualities of a challenge buddy and examples of encouraging statements can be on hand or posted in the classroom.

3. Once this is achieved, the class is divided in half. One group will be naming a challenge they would like help with and then being matched up with a willing challenge buddy.

4. As each child is given a buddy, the pair is free to go off to an area they choose for their working spot.

5. Children will finish at different times, but aim for about 30 to 40 minutes, to allow ample time for switching so the other half will have time to work on their challenges.

6. Allow time after a Challenge Circle for comments from the children regarding how things went, how they felt, or strategies used by the challenge buddies. This is a satisfying way to culminate a Challenge Day.

Some children will have a very clear and often ingenious method for helping their friend, while others may need a few leading suggestions. For the most part, the children seem to need very little guidance during this process. In fact, expect some very touching and surprising interchanges among the students. This is a wonderful time for teachers to observe the children in loving action with their classmates or to give needed support if there is any unkindness. It will also make apparent the level of emotional safety in the classroom community and reveal any areas for improvement.

Later on, choose to orchestrate this event differently to allow more time for one half of the students to have their experience on a separate day and then follow up with the next group later in the week. This exercise is meant more as an introduction and a way of showcasing both aspects of getting or giving help regarding a challenge, rather than really improving anyone's skills at this point.

One of our first Challenge Days yielded many touching anecdotes. A child who had a longstanding challenge with body skills was partnered with a particularly talented athlete. The "challenge buddy" had taken his partner out to a protected area of pine trees to teach him some tricks about how to kick a soccer ball. Whooshing by on my way to check out how the rest of the groups were doing with their respective partners, I casually asked, "How's it going?" The "coach" responded with a most enthusiastic, utterly sincere and emphatic, "He's doing great!!" My heart warmed with the thought, "This is actually really working!" A few moments later the speech teacher came into my room looking amazed and saying, "I just saw the most wonderful interaction just now…" I said, "Yes we're having a Challenge Day. Look over there—someone is showing this child how to start a story." With that, the teacher's eyes welled up and she had to leave the room because she was so moved by what was happening. It had even more meaning for her because she had personally worked with both children in the soccer kicking pair and knew what it would mean for the challenge partner to receive such a positive compliment from his challenge buddy.

How Often To Do the "Days"?

If you do one Gifts and Challenges Introductory Day (this could be one morning or one day), then follow up with a role playing to introduce the Comparison Jungle (20 minutes), and then one Challenge Day (one morning or afternoon), it is enough to create a strong enough presence for these ideas to flourish in your class. To keep these ideas current throughout the year, make certain to use and integrate the terms frequently and naturally. Remember also to disclose your own challenges and share some concrete examples of your gifts. You will make a very strong impression on your students through your honesty and willingness to share.

Ideally, if you could do two gift days and two challenge days or choose one extension or variation per year, it would be most effective and satisfying for the children. If you have a multi-age classroom, you can capitalize on the fact that your older students know the ropes and they will help you with discussion times, role playing, and reminding you that "We need to do Gifts and Challenges."

There are many other ideas for integrating into your classrooms to be found in Section: 4 on Creativity. Even though we all feel a pull and push to keep to the academic schedule, when you go off the beaten path it is so rewarding for the students and a beautiful shot in the arm for you as their teacher. It's why we do the work! It is enlivening and inspiring in unexpected ways and will pay off when the children and you must go back to the normal routine. You will notice how the ideas begin to spontaneously show up in the children's conversations and interactions throughout the year.

Section 4: Creativity

The Children Have Ideas!

The initial experience was so positive for both the students and their teachers. We had done one Gifts Day and one Challenges Day that first year. We thought we were complete and felt the satisfaction of a lesson well received. What happened next was unexpected but shouldn't have been. The children began to make suggestions and requests. Most of these revolved around the Creating and Body categories. "For the Next Gifts Day, (what next Gifts Day?) the children asked, could they bring in things from home?" "Could they bring their guitar, their violin, their scooters, a puzzle, a skateboard, a bike, a keyboard?" The answer to all of these questions ultimately turned out to be yes. The following examples did not occur on one day or even in one year, but they all happened.

The guitarists were seated outside on the lawn, the violinists walked around playing their tunes in the midst of the other activities, the puzzle experts set up in the middle of the floor; we had a keyboard which got set up in the corner of the classroom surrounded by a small audience of fellow pianists and listeners.

As for the wheels…it was daunting for obvious reasons, but we got permission and scores of children brought in bikes, rollerblades, or scooters for a Gifts Day primarily focused on a group ride around the perimeter of the blacktop. Children shared their particular form of wheels with those who didn't bring anything. They taught and coached others who had never tried a particular item. Then they finished and went on to do other gifts! It was unbelievable! Things went smoothly, no one got hurt, the children helped each other, and they were thrilled! They had thought of it and asked for it and it worked. Gifts and Challenges was no longer my brainchild. It now belonged to them.

More Ideas

There are so many possibilities for extending this work and thereby keeping the concepts alive for the children. Just when it seems there is nothing more to explore, things reveal themselves in a new way. It truly is an on-going collaborative work.

On other "gift days," we set up a table for preparing a fruit salad. One child stayed there the whole time—she loved cooking so much she said, "I just couldn't leave!" The teacher who had a gift for cooking made apple turnovers with the children. Another time we emphasized science for a particular student who adored and excelled in that area, so another teacher made up a series of science experiments that he or anyone else could easily do.

Then we began to try isolating one aspect of the charts and did a nature day. The children set up bird blinds with blankets and sticks, they collected leaves, they drew flowers, they observed insects, they climbed trees (with a teacher nearby of course), they went on a nature hunt, and they made artistic creations from natural materials—sticks, rocks, weeds, and seed pods. The children actually looked at and communed with the natural world.

At work time, we tried out the idea of choosing a gift to exercise on one day and a challenge to practice on another day. We wrote these down on our work plans.

We tried the idea of choosing one gift in the Thinking area and did an experiment to see how long we could concentrate. That was incredibly successful (see the following write-up on Concentration). Then we thought we would also try to do that with a challenge as well. Throughout the week, the children kept reminding me that we needed to do that Challenge Day. They were really invested in seeing the outcome of their experiment.

Judy Donovan

The Concentration Experiment

One weekend in May, while exercising my sometimes neglected gift for drawing, some resistance to finishing came up for me. Using pen and ink to illustrate a waterfall, there was one last corner at the top that I was avoiding. I brought it to school on Monday in order to point out my challenge for drawing water. It was a perfect way to talk about challenges "within" your gifts and to show the children how that issue might be approached.

As we were discussing the topic, the idea of concentration was mentioned. It was the ideal moment to introduce a thought that had come to me the night before. We would each choose one Thinking Gift and set out to concentrate for as long as we could on that one thing or area. We would do it as an experiment and just see what we might be capable of, by giving our best effort.

The following is a letter describing to parents how the experiment went that day.

Dear Parents,

In the last few weeks, our class has made some amazing discoveries about our concentration abilities. We decided to try an experiment. We each chose one Thinking Gift and set out to concentrate for as long as we could on that one thing or area. I chose my Gift for drawing (even though it was in the Creative category) and as we got underway, sat down to work along with the children. Once everyone had their choices set up it became unusually quiet in the room.

I wondered if another teacher was telling the children to be quiet. This was not so because the teachers were very involved in their own class projects at the time. I wondered if a child had written "silence" on the board (an exercise we do every Wednesday to see how long it takes the class to become completely still for a few moments). Not so. Then I got back to my own concentrating. I thought, "This can't last very much longer." But it did.

This beautiful, deep concentration lasted for 65 minutes. The quality of the work was gorgeous. The enthusiasm for the work was inspiring. As the morning progressed I invited our administrators to come in and look. The children didn't really notice, they just kept on working. At the end of the morning there was a sense of satisfaction and calm that was palpable. We wanted to share our work with each other, so we did that at Circle. They all seemed so pleased with themselves.

We did the same thing the next day, with a difference. We said that if you needed a break for a snack or if you were losing your concentration, you could run a lap on the field. This change caused many children to get too excited about running on the field with a friend, so our second day was not as magical as the first day. We laughed at ourselves and realized that this is just human nature. But we remembered our day of triumph.

We talked about the little girl in one of Maria Montessori's classrooms back in Italy almost 100 years ago. This child of three or four was concentrating so deeply on the cylinder blocks that the teacher was able to pick her up – chair, table, and all -- yet she remained absorbed in doing her work. We wondered if we would be able to do that well.

We also decided that we would try this same concentrating idea the next week, only focusing on one of our challenges for as long as we could. Challenges are different in that we can choose a challenge buddy to help us if we need it. This day also had its magic. Again, there was lovely concentration, clever strategies for helping each other, and determined students who decided to face their challenges alone.

Later that week we had a class discussion about the qualities of concentration. We are not finished yet. The children have so many ideas and insights to share. We're writing them down so we can go back to them when we need inspiration.

Presenting Gifts and Challenges to Kindergarteners

When thinking about how to present these concepts to younger children, how to proceed initially seemed a bit unclear. Late in the previous spring, while sharing with my class the idea of making a Gifts and Challenges journal for the Kindergarteners, I held up the new journal for them to see. In the midst of musing aloud about how it might go, Martin, one of my quieter students, quickly raised his hand. He asked in utter seriousness, "So when are "we" going to teach it to them?" His earnest and literal interpretation of himself and his classmates as the Kindergarteners' potential teachers was very touching, but seemed like just another one of those cute anecdotes to tell my staff after class. I did share it later with my fellow teachers, who all thought it was just *darling*, and then it was simply forgotten.

As the day for the presentation approached, I was nervous about giving the lesson since my years as a preschool teacher were far behind me. Recapturing the special touch required to speak the younger children's language and captivate their attention for such an abstract idea seemed difficult and perhaps not really at their level.

As I rushed to gather the lesson materials and was about to go out the door, I noticed Martin. He was sitting at his table, head bowed, fervently concentrating on an assignment. This was enough to jog my memory and inspire me at the same instant. "Come with me, it's time to teach the kindergarteners," I whispered into his ear. He came to attention immediately and helped me quickly rustle up the other willing volunteers. They were only too happy to drop what they were doing for such an "important mission." We pranced down the sidewalk to our destination, full of whispered excitement and the wonderful anticipation that being of true help can bring.

How It Went

1. **We gathered at Circle with the Kindergarteners. The Gifts and Challenges idea was introduced by showing a large version of the logo.**

   "The sun represents our gifts—what you are already good at, while the mountain makes us think of our challenges—what is hard for you or takes more practice. The wavy lines stand for the river which reminds us of life. The whole picture means that in life everybody has gifts and challenges."

2. **Each older student was asked to name one of his or her gifts and one of his or her challenges.**

This would be the link-in for the younger children to start thinking more concretely about this topic. "My gift is reading, and my challenge is handwriting." said Kiran. "My gift is math, and my challenge is paying attention." said Eli. The Kindergarteners were riveted. Watching their reactions, you could almost hear them thinking, *"What!? They're telling us what they're good at and what they're* ***not*** *good at! It must be safe to do that!"*

3. **Each older student was paired with a Kindergartener for the purpose of helping the kindergarteners fill out their Gifts and Challenges charts**.

For this younger age child, the charts consist of pictures with a box next to each one. The child then draws an image of the sun to indicate a gift or a mountain to show a challenge. The older students were close at hand to keep the task going and to read labels or identify any pictures that were not obvious to their younger partners.

Once the activity was underway, the older children were heard softly explaining what a picture meant, or sweetly asking questions.

"So do you think puzzles are a gift or a challenge for you?" "Okay, now make a sun or a mountain right next to it."

One kindergartener said, "Since I was a baby I could always draw circles, and I was so good at them!"

Another said, "It's hard to climb trees, but I like it!"

"Are you good at being gentle?" asked an older boy, "it's like..." and the younger boy responded, "soft!"

An older student continued coaching, "Let's do "Creating" now... "Are you good at drawing?" Younger student, "I'm so good at art!"

Another older student was working with the care of animals section, "So do you love your dog, Max?" The child nodded yes, "Let's put a sun because you love him very much."

Towards the end of the activity, one little child cheerfully wondered if we were "going to do our challenges today too?"

It was so gratifying to see the younger children already deeply engaged with this process and the older ones taking on the role of being the Kindergarteners trusted guides with such sincerity. This delightful interchange lasted about 15 to 20 minutes.

Not far into this part of the lesson, we realized that something special was afoot. We wanted to discreetly capture some of it on film, but had not thought to bring a camera or a means to videotape. (We did manage to take a few photos of the children with their partners and only wished we could have taped their verbal interactions as well. If you try it, be sure to have some means on hand to record these special moments for parents and teachers.)

4. As each partnership finished the charts at a different moment, **the natural next step was for each younger student to show their older partner one of their gifts from among the classroom materials**.

   The older students showed respect, gentle encouragement, and genuine enthusiasm for the accomplishments of the younger children.

   As our time with the Kindergarteners came to a close, we all felt elated by what had just happened. As we strolled back down the sidewalk, we chattered with animation among ourselves about what each younger child said or did during "our" lesson.

   The serendipity of this lesson turned out to be a beautiful way to introduce these ideas to the next generation of lower elementary students. The experience served as another reminder that "following the child" often yields the most elegant answer to the question of "How can this lesson best be taught to the students?" The act of trusting the children and then being willing to let them take the lead, gives rise to those unexpected shining moments in teaching, which are so illuminating for the students and rewarding for their teachers.

Section 5: Materials and Ideas for In-Depth Work

Gifts and Challenges: Self Reflections for the Older Elementary Student

"You can't give your gift away to someone else, but you can share it. You can't make your challenge go away by wishing, but you can practice until it gets easier or perhaps becomes a talent."

Please write a full explanation of what may happen

…if you have a gift and don't use it:

____

____

…if you have a challenge and give up:

____

____

…if you have a gift and use it to make others feel bad:

____

____

…if you have a challenge and use it to make yourself feel bad:

____

____

…if you have a gift and use it and enjoy it:

____

____

…if you have a gift and share it:

____

____

…if you have a challenge and practice it:

____

____

…if you have a challenge and show others how you got better:

____

____

…if (your idea)

____

____

Discussion Prompts for Deeper Thinking

Gifts are to honor, exercise, share

Ways to honor your gifts

- Gratitude
- Exercising your gifts regularly
- Showing another your process

Ways to honor others' gifts

- Admire
- Encourage
- Express curiosity about the other person's process
- Acknowledge the other person's progress, product, courage

Ways to exercise your gifts

- Keep track of how often you remember to use and develop your gift
- Set aside special, uninterrupted time for your gift
- Find a friend, mentor, or teacher who understands and supports your gift

Inner Preparation

- Set goals for your gifts
- Prioritize–which gift will you do first?
- Inspiration–what inspires you to exercise your gift?

- Self-validation; are you able to kindly acknowledge yourself as you exercise your gift?

- Inner emotional safety; do you know when you are criticizing yourself or when you are accepting yourself? Do you know how to get out of the Comparison Jungle once you know you are there?

Outer Preparation

- Make sure you have the right materials, enough materials

- Make sure your space is set up well

- Make sure your materials are organized

- Make sure you have set aside enough time

Ways to share your gifts

A result of exercising your gift could be:

- Shared verbally with a friend as you experience your gift

- Shared visually as you experience your gift

- Shared at Circle, either visually or verbally

- Shared with parents as a product to take home

Challenges are to accept, practice, share

Ways to accept your challenges

- Realize that everyone has challenges

- Trust that with practice and help you can improve

- Welcome the challenge as an opportunity to develop courage and perseverance

- Discover the hidden gift within the challenge

- Remember how it feels to conquer a challenge
- Realize and trust that others want us to succeed
- Realize the contribution you make to the world when you are applying yourself with determination and exercising your "will"

<u>Ways to accept others' challenges</u>

- Encourage someone who is frustrated
- Offer to help as a challenge buddy
- Recognize that you have your own challenges
- Be patient and tolerant toward someone's challenge
- Acknowledge or compliment courage and determination

<u>Ideas about challenges</u>

- You have a **right** to receive help
- You have a **responsibility** to meet your challenge vs. avoiding, pretending you don't have it, hiding from it, or feeling ashamed of it
- You have an inner call to **rise** to a challenge

<u>Ways to practice a challenge</u>

- Keep track of how often you practice a challenge
- Set aside special uninterrupted time to practice
- Find a trustworthy challenge buddy

<u>Inner Preparation</u>

- Name the challenge

- Set a goal for your challenge
- Reward yourself and acknowledge yourself
- Motivation–what motivates you to face a challenge?
- Inner emotional safety; have you read the "**Rights to Emotional Safety**" before you practice your challenge?
- Have you read your **Inspirational Quotes** for courage or remembered an inspiring story about someone else who has faced his or her challenge?
- Do you know how to fully acknowledge yourself or ask for support when you need it?
- Do you know how to tell if you are in the Comparison Jungle and how to get out if you are there?

<u>Outer Preparation</u>

- Keep a record of challenges that you would like to work on
- Choose a trustworthy challenge buddy
- Break down challenges into smaller steps with a challenge buddy or a teacher
- Set up breaks if you need them
- Set up time chunks with rewards or talks with a support person before and after facing the challenge
- Decide to work on your challenge alone or with a challenge buddy

<u>Ways to share a challenge</u>

- Decide on the triumph, process, or result to be shared
- Decide if you will share privately with a teacher/trusted friend or with the whole group at Circle

- Tell your goal regarding your challenge
- Introduce your challenge buddy
- Describe your particular challenge
- Share the steps you took in your challenge session

Share the results including frustrations, feelings, improvements, new realizations, ah-ha moments, triumphs, successes, small victories.

Tell whether you would try a new approach next time or if you would repeat the same approach many times.

Do you think it would work to use the memory of this time to help you when you are working by yourself on the same or another challenge?

Choose volunteer scribes to write down the challenge sharing ideas for the student who is speaking.

Ask if there are students who would like to compliment (regarding courage) the child who has faced a challenge.

Guides to Emotional Self-Defense

In this section, children are given ways to think about their emotions as they affect their approach to learning as well as tools to address emotional stumbling blocks as they arise. These difficulties may come from other students or from within the child's own thinking patterns. The importance of being emotionally available to learn is stressed in Priscilla Vail's book called *Emotion: The On/Off Switch to Learning,* 1994. The more clarity children can be given to help them understand what might be interfering with their learning process, the better equipped they will be to make the most of their gifts and to accept their challenges as opportunities.

There is a general checklist called Rights to Emotional Safety which is also included as a part of the Gifts and Challenges Journal. This is useful for a child to read privately at needed intervals or as a jumping off point during a class discussion. The checklist could be hung as a poster in the classroom to be introduced at the beginning of the year.

This material also contains a review of the concept of the Comparison Jungle, with sample thoughts or feelings that can get in the way when one is in a comparing state of mind.

For additional support, there are two guided helping sessions and one to be used independently. These are designed for sorting out problems between children or getting to the crux of one's own negative thought patterns. These procedures are more time consuming, yet could prove invaluable in cases that might need more specific intervention.

Emotional Safety: Exposing the Inner Bully

How to Know When You are in the Comparison Jungle

1. You are in the **Comparison Jungle** when you are working on an activity and, at the same time, comparing yourself to others instead of concentrating and enjoying your own work.

2. You are in the **Comparison Jungle** when you are looking at what you have accomplished and unkindly comparing yourself to what others have accomplished, instead of appreciating what you have done and being pleased with your own progress.

Comparison Put downs from Yourself

You might be saying things to yourself like:

1. "I should know this already. If it's easy for my friend, it should be easy for me."

2. "If I don't know now, I'll never get it."

3. "I haven't been good at this before, which means I'll never be good at it."

4. "Everybody else can do this, why can't I?"

Examples of how it Feels to be in the Comparison Jungle

1. Negative thoughts like, "I'll never be able to do this."
2. Self put downs like, "I must not be as smart as other kids."
3. Feeling defeated; not even trying to understand.
4. Feeling overwhelmed; feeling that there are too many parts to understand.
5. Feeling frozen; like you can't remember anything or what to do next.
6. Feeling panicked; having butterflies in your stomach or a headache or that you would like to run away.
7. Feeling fearful; that you might never be able to do it, that there is something wrong with you.
8. Self-doubting; believing that you are not able to learn fast enough or well enough.
9. Being tearful; feeling that you might cry whenever you start to do your challenge.
10. Believing negative comments; if someone says something unkind about your abilities, being sure that they are right.
11. Re-playing past mistakes; thinking about times that were difficult over and over as you are about to try your challenge.
12. Comparing yourself to others; wanting to avoid your challenge by eating, talking, wandering, dawdling.

Self Put-downs

How to ask for Support When You are in the Comparison Jungle

1. If you think you are struggling with self put downs, ask for a helping session with a teacher or a challenge buddy.
2. Choose a time for the session.

3. Choose a private place for your session.

4. Once your session is finished, write your feelings or inspiring quotes in your Gifts and Challenges Journal.

Encouraging Thoughts to Replace Self Put-downs

1. I am essential. (This means we cannot do without you.)

2. My gifts are valuable.

3. It is right and safe for me to be in the process of learning.

4. It is ok to not know everything.

5. Everyone has challenges just as I do.

6. Everyone has gifts just as I do.

7. What I have to offer is important and needed.

8. I trust in my place and my purpose.

9. The people who love and support me are:

   ____

   ____

10. My quotes for inspiration and courage are:

   ____

   ____

   ____

   ____

   ____

Guidelines for a Helping Session With Self Put Downs

Steps to Identify, Understand, Forgive, Clear, Inspire

1. The teacher and/or challenge buddy invites the child to use the feelings wheel to identify feelings.

2. The teacher and/or challenge buddy invites the child to identify the type of self put downs that are causing difficulty.

3. The teacher and/or challenge buddy shows understanding by sharing a time when he or she felt the same.

4. The teacher and/or challenge buddy invites the child to feel compassion for self and all others who have felt the same (spend a quiet moment on this).

5. The teacher and/or challenge buddy invites the child to forgive themselves for the self put downs and for giving them too much power (the child says aloud or writes in journal, "I forgive myself for…").

6. The teacher and/or challenge buddy invites the child to use a technique for releasing the negative thoughts and clearing the mind… breathing, balloon, or a kind helper. a. Take a deep breath and see all the negative thoughts gently blowing away. b. Put the thoughts in a black balloon and see them float away. c. Imagine a kind helper sweeping the thoughts from your mind.

7. The child says aloud any courageous statement which inspires him or her to remember his or her right to inner emotional safety.

8. The teacher and/or challenge buddy asks the child whether he or she is ready to face the challenge on his or her own, or if he or she would like help from a challenge buddy.

Steps to take on your own with Self Put Downs

1. Use the feelings wheel to identify your feelings.

2. Write these feelings and self put downs in your Gifts and Challenges Journal.

3. Spend a few quiet moments to realize that you are not alone in these thoughts and to feel understanding and compassion for yourself and all others.

4. Use a technique for clearing your mind: a. Take a deep breath and see all the negative thoughts gently blowing away. b. Put the thoughts in a black balloon and see them float away. c. Imagine a kind helper sweeping the thoughts from your mind.

5. Read the Encouraging Thoughts.

6. Write down some Encouraging Thoughts.

7. Read the quote that you use for courage and inspiration.

8. Try again. Face your challenge on your own.

Three Things to Tell Yourself After a Self Put down

1. I deserve to treat myself kindly.

2. I deserve to feel safe with my thoughts.

3. I can use my own power to protect myself from negative thoughts.

Emotional Safety: Handling Put downs from Others

How to Tell When Your Emotional Safety is not Being Respected

1. Someone has given you a comparison put down about your work.

2. Someone doubts in your ability to try something new.

3. Someone is telling you they are better than you.

4. Someone is telling you that you should be doing better or be farther along than you are.

5. Someone wants you to race with them or is trying to convince you that working fast is better than working carefully and enjoying your work.

6. Someone is asking you about your progress in a "comparing" instead of a "caring" way.

7. Someone is giving you too much help because they think you can't do it by yourself.

8. Someone is often telling you how and when to do things.

9. Someone is telling you that they won't be your friend unless…

10. Someone is trying to get you to do things that you don't want to do.

How to Ask for a Helping Session—Handling Put Downs from Others

1. Ask a teacher to stand by while you give an "I Message" to the child.

2. Ask for a helping session with the child and the teacher.

3. Ask for a helping session with only the teacher.

Guidelines for a Helping Session When Emotional Safety is Disrespected

1. The child who has been disrespected is invited to use the Feelings Wheel and give an "I Message."

2. The teacher shows understanding and empathy.

3. The common reasons for disrespect are given in a gentle tone (jealousy, one-upmanship, Comparison Jungle thoughts, believing you have to be "better than" to feel good about yourself…).

4. The teacher asks the second child if he or she can think of a way to make amends and regain trust.

5. The teacher invites input from the first child (receiver). The teacher invites input from the second child.

6. The first child is invited to make a genuine positive statement about the second child if ready. If so, the teacher repeats and embellishes.

7. The teacher closes the session by reading or inviting the children to read the Rights to Emotional Safety.

Rights to Emotional Safety

1. I have a right to be treated kindly.

2. I have a right to feel safe while I am learning.

3. I have a right to be respected for my Gifts and Challenges.

4. I have a right to work at my own pace.

5. I have a right to work in my own way.

6. I have a right to ask for help if I really need it.

7. I have a right to respectfully say no to help.

8. I have a right to ask for support for my challenges.

9. I have a right to ask for encouragement with my gifts.

10. I have a right to stand up for myself firmly and kindly.

Three Things to Tell Yourself When Your Emotional Safety Has Been Disrespected

1. I deserve respect.

2. I deserve to feel safe while I am learning.

3. I can use my own power to protect myself by reading the Encouraging Thoughts, by asking for a Helping Session, by going to a teacher for help in giving an "I Message," or by using my Gifts and Challenges Journal and reading my quotes for courage and inspiration.

Section 6: Additional Material for Teachers

Included in this section are further notes on the peace activities, thoughts on parent involvement, questionnaires, evaluations, a list of quotes, and an essay on bullying.

Ideas for Peace Shelf

1. **Gifts and Challenges cards derived from the Gifts and Challenges Chart**

   Goal: to foster peaceful qualities by giving concrete actions which children can practice during the school day

   Materials: a selection of cards from the People and Kindnesses categories

   Activity:
   - The child may choose a card to "practice." For example, on the generosity card are listed examples of possible generous actions that could be done at school.

- The child can then choose a time to perform the action and optionally record this in their Gifts and Challenges Journal.

- Alternately, a list of the qualities in each category and ideas for practicing them could be made available for reference after the child has chosen a card from the People or Kindness set.

2. **Nature Walks**

Goal: to foster a connection to nature by providing direct and solitary contact with natural surroundings

Materials: a necklace or pass with a beautiful scene from nature (photo or drawing)

Activity:
- If older students are available, they could act as the "guide" or supervisor during this five to ten minute experience. The younger student lets the "guide" know they are going on their nature walk. The timer is set, and the older student observes from a distance. The guide will then greet the student and participate in a brief sharing exercise concerning what was seen or felt on the nature walk.

3. **Feelings Cards**

Goal: to gain familiarity with the Feelings vocabulary and practice in identifying personal feelings

Materials: cards which illustrate all the feelings, labels for **Comfortable** and **Uncomfortable**, label for **What I Am Feeling Today**

Activity:
- The child can sort the cards into the two categories and then choose from those sets which reflect their current feelings. Journaling any thoughts or recording feelings in their Gifts and Challenges Journal is a further extension of this activity.

4. Needs Cards

Goal: to gain practice in learning the common needs of people and sorting into types of needs, as well as identifying their own current needs

Materials: cards for each need, labels for sorting Needs Cards (**Physical**, **Feelings**, **Learning**, and **Inspirational**), a Needs Wheel for identifying personal needs, gems for placing on the Needs Wheel

Activity:

- The child can study the Needs Wheel, then using the cards, sort according to types of Needs, then place the gems on the chart for identifying personal needs. Journaling can be used for identifying needs in a specific situation or in a pre-written hypothetical situation.

5. Labyrinth Walk or Small Hand-Held Labyrinth

Goal: to give structured time for quiet reflection

Materials: Labyrinth (if available) or it can be easily constructed with small stones as a class project

Activity:

- The child chooses the labyrinth necklace and lets a teacher know when he or she will start. The walk can be done with no specific intention or can also be used as a tool for inspiration.

No Intention: Walk slowly and notice your natural surroundings – trees, flowers, birds, wind…

For inspiration: Before you start your walk, think about something you need help with, then begin your walk.

At the end of your walk see if you have a new idea about your problem or need.

Alternate activity: The small labyrinth is available on the Peace shelf or in the Peace Corner. The same two approaches can be used.

6. The Feelings Wheels and Needs Wheel

Goal: to give time with each wheel in order to familiarize with the Feelings vocabulary and Needs terminology.

Materials: Feelings Wheel, Needs Wheel, and colored gems for placement on the wheels

Activity: The child reads the wheels and places gems on personal feelings or needs that apply for the moment or to a specific issue the child is revisiting

Selection of Inspirational Quotes

These quotes can be used for the journal section on quotes for courage and determination. They can also serve as a starter collection if you wish to use them at a peace circle or in a general discussion on how to encourage yourself or others.

"Help the next person who needs some minor assistance."

"Love your neighbor as yourself."

"Ever tried. Ever failed. No matter. Try again. Fail again. Fail better."

"Bravery is believing in yourself, and that thing nobody can teach you."

"The most wasted day of all is that in which we have not laughed."

"Wise and slow, they stumble that run fast."

"Cherish animals."

"Hope is the thing with feathers-that perches in the soul-and sings the tune without the words-and never stops –at all."

"Honesty is the best policy."

"Never discourage anyone who continually makes progress, no matter how slow."

"Rise to your challenges, don't fear them." (student)

"It is easier to begin well, than to finish well."

"Someone who seems different may have amazing ideas." (student)

"Down in their hearts, wise men and women know this truth: the only way to help yourself is to help others."

"You can't succeed if you don't get out and try."

"If you ever need a helping hand, it is at the end of your arm. As you get older you must remember you have a second hand. The first one is to help yourself. The second hand is to help others."

"Be flexible."

"The only people who never fail are those who never try."

Ideas for Parent Involvement

After each Gifts and Challenges Day, a letter is sent home which explains the array of experiences that were had by the children on that particular day. This communication provides a chance to review the basic concepts for the parents. It invites parents to look at their copies of the child's chart and hopefully engage the child in a conversation about the child's choices or the parent's own gifts and challenges—either from when they were children or now as adults. Included is a sample letter for your own adaptation.

Dear Parents,

Recently the children had a lesson called Gifts and Challenges. This lesson came about as a response to a child who was comparing himself to other students and feeling like he was not working on the "right" materials. I am including the short version of the lesson for you because it seemed to meet a deep need within the children. They became very excited when the other teachers and I shared our own gifts and challenges. When this topic comes up at home, it will be useful for the parents and teachers to speak about the subject in a similar way. The lesson is as follows:

"When you are born, you have certain gifts—things that will be very easy for you, very fun, and don't take a lot of practice. These gifts are yours to use and to share. Also, you have certain

challenges—things that need lots of practice and are not fun at first. Sometimes you just don't want to do these things but need to try. <u>These challenges are yours to practice and make better</u>. Everyone has both gifts and challenges.

There is no one who has all gifts and no challenges, and no one who has all challenges and no gifts. Everyone is special and unique—that is what makes everyone valuable and important.

You can't give your gift to someone else, but you can share it. You can't make your challenge go away by wishing, but it can get easier by practicing.

If you weren't born with a certain gift, you can practice until that skill becomes a talent—something you're very good at.

If you are working on a challenge, it can get much easier, stay a bit of a challenge, or slowly get better and better if you practice."

You have choices about what you do with your gifts and challenges.

<u>Gifts</u>

You could have a gift and use it and enjoy it.

You could share your gift.

You could have a gift and not use it.

You could use your gift to make others feel bad.

<u>Challenges</u>

You could have a challenge and practice it.

If you have a challenge, you could show others how you got better.

You could have a challenge and never practice it.

You could have a challenge and use it to make yourself feel bad.

In class, we talked about these choices and what would be encouraging and discouraging about both. Each child shared with me a chart of his or her gifts. That chart is attached. Please talk with your child about this list. It is very informative and should generate an interesting discussion.

If you have any questions or uncover any valuable information which could help me, please share!

A more detailed introductory letter is also an option:

For Parents: How a Gifts and Challenges Day Works

This is a more detailed description of a Gifts and Challenges day, which I hope will make your understanding of your child's experience more concrete and meaningful.

We have already set the stage for the event by letting the students know in advance exactly when we will be having a Gifts and Challenges Day. It is very important to try for full attendance as it is such a foundational lesson and vital to the emotional climate of the classroom. Since the older returning students are "in the know," there is usually quite a bit of excitement in anticipation of the "Day." Older students are asked not to say too much about it to the new students, since we'd like there to be the most impact possible upon their first hearing of the "Story of Gifts and Challenges."

Once the children and teachers are gathered at Circle, the history of Gifts and Challenges is told as an oral story with lots of expression and drama. Those who have heard the story before are "helping" with knowing looks, laughter, sympathetic murmurs, and lots of head-nodding empathy sprinkled throughout the "telling."

Immediately following this, I give the lesson which explains what Gifts and Challenges are, using personal examples as well as typical classroom scenarios to engage the children.

Following this, I share with the class regarding each of my own Gifts and Challenges. Wall charts are used which list 6 different categories, with many items under each heading.

The categories are: Thinking, Creating, Body, Kindnesses, People, and Nature.

In taking the first "turn" I use this as an **opportunity to model healthy self-acknowledgment regarding my gifts and matter of fact self-acceptance**

regarding my challenges. As the model, I offer lightly humorous comments to accompany the process of filling out the charts, which helps each child understand that this is a safe, enjoyable activity.

The fascination the children show as they observe each teacher fill out the charts is always evident. This comes through in their spontaneous comments and the obvious joy and curiosity on their faces, as they witness their teachers reveal themselves with such honesty and warmth.

Somewhere in the midst of the teachers' process, the children start to visibly vibrate in anticipation of filling out their own charts, which are provided for them in paper format. Once these precious papers are passed out, the children are completely engrossed: heads down with intense concentration, talking with animation about one of their Gifts, asking a teacher what one of the items means, or nonchalantly naming a Challenge.

Younger students are helped with reading and filling out their charts if needed. When all the children have completed their charts we gather together to talk about what activities have been set up on the tables and to go over a few ground rules for the smooth functioning of the day.

One of the most important aspects of this process is the uninterrupted time component. The children need the reassurance that they will have the freedom to not only choose what they are going to do, but that they will have ample time in which to explore and practice their Gifts.

We teachers and parents are often tempted to orchestrate or manage time and activities, since that is such an integral and often necessary part of our job as their guides. However, it is a very powerful and moving moment when you witness the visible sigh of relief as it truly registers with the children that they will certainly have more than enough time to do what they love and what they are good at!

Next, the children are set free to choose their activities. Teachers or helpers are stationed indoors and out, in order to help facilitate and give general supervision. **Most importantly, the teachers and helpers are there as admiring witnesses to the wonderful talents and unexpected creativity brought forth by this unusual day.** We work through the morning, and in the afternoon we continue for a while, to make sure everyone feels satisfied and complete in terms of time.

Ideally, there will be a final wrap-up Circle for talking about which Gifts we exercised or giving time for those who are excited to show the class some of their creations.

All too soon, it is time to go home. Hopefully, you will catch some of the enthusiasm the children felt as they experienced their first Gifts and Challenges lesson of the year.

Letter to Kindergarten Parents: Explanation of Gifts and Challenges Introduction

Dear Kindergarten Parents,

I recently had the privilege of presenting the Gifts and Challenges lesson to your children. I was assisted by several elementary students while the preschool teachers observed and lent their support for the follow-up activity.

The lesson was a brief introduction to the idea that everyone is born with gifts and challenges. The older students shared one gift and one challenge that they each have. This moment seemed to be quite interesting and compelling for the kindergartners. It provided a perfect opening for these older students to become the guides for each of your kindergarteners as they went through their own Gifts and Challenges Journals.

In looking at your child's journal, you will see that gifts are represented by a sun, while challenges are represented by a mountain. When you go through these journals with your child, it can be a wonderful insight into their own self-perceptions at this time and a great opportunity for extended conversation. It can also be a great way to share what some of your own gifts or challenges were as a child, or even some that you now have as an adult.

We do this lesson every year in lower elementary, so we will continue to have wonderful opportunities to practice and discuss the many aspects of this important life lesson.

I am so grateful for the chance to share this with your students and hope that you will find these ideas helpful in talking with your children about school or family life.

Other Suggestions for Parent Involvement

- Use a parent questionnaire (Table 6-2) after a few Gifts and Challenges days have occurred in your classroom.

- Show the Gifts and Challenges DVD at a parent meeting, or individual copies may be made available for each family.

- Use conferences as an opportunity for coaching parents in the use of these concepts at home. By repeating the vocabulary and using a calm, matter of fact tone with their children while reminding them that we all have gifts and challenges, many frustrations and melt-downs around homework or other tasks can be averted and turned into a positive interchange.

- Give a mini workshop on Gifts and Challenges for Parents—parents fill out their own charts and discussion follows with tips for integrating ideas at home.

- Give parents suggestions for practicing gifts with their child or tackling a family challenge together on the weekend.

Table 6-1: Children's Questionnaire—Gifts and Challenges

1. Do you like the Gifts and Challenges Days? □ Yes □ No
2. If yes, why do you like them?

   ____
   ____
   ____

3. If you don't like them, please tell why not.

   ____
   ____
   ____

4. Is there something you wish would happen differently on Gifts and Challenges Days?

   ____
   ____
   ____

5. How often would you like to have Gifts and Challenges Days?

   ____
   ____
   ____

6. How do you feel when you get to do your gifts?

   ____
   ____
   ____

7. How do you feel when you are practicing a challenge?

   ____
   ____
   ____

8. The last time we had a Gifts and Challenges Day, what gifts did you exercise?

   ____
   ____
   ____

9. The last time we had a Challenge Day, which challenge did you practice?

   ____

____

____

____

10. Do you feel safe to learn new things in our classroom?

____

____

____

11. Do you feel safe to admit your challenges?

____

____

____

12. Do you feel safe to share your gifts?

____

____

____

13. Do you have any suggestions about Gifts and Challenges days?

____

____

____

14. Do you have any suggestions about Challenge days?

____

____

____

Table 6-2: Questionnaire for Parents—Gifts and Challenges

1. Did you sit down with your child and look at the Gifts and Challenges Chart together?
   □ Yes □ No □ Intend to
2. Did you share any of your own gifts and challenges with your child?
   □ Yes □ No □ Intend to □ Not Sure How To
3. Have you had opportunities or occasions to use the Gifts and Challenges terms to help your child in situations at home or regarding schoolwork, self-confidence, etc.?
   □ Yes □ No □ Intend to □ Not Sure How To Implement □ Would Like Concrete Suggestions or Examples

4. Do you believe using this terminology/concept with your child could be helpful?
   □ Yes □ No □ Not Sure of Application
5. Would you like more information on how the actual presentation is done?
   □ Yes □ No □ I Feel I Understand Enough
6. If you do want more information, check what you would like (please check all that apply):
   □ A write-up of the story, the day's activities, etc.
   □ A copy of the DVD
   □ A Parents' Workshop
7. Questions/Comments

   ____
   ____
   ____
   ____

Table 6-3: Teacher Questionnaire—Gifts and Challenges

1. How many Gifts and Challenges Days have you implemented?

   ____
   ____
   ____

2. Did you re-tell the story from the outline? Did you make personal modifications? Please explain.

   ____
   ____
   ____

3. Did you disclose your own gifts and challenges? Please explain.

   ____
   ____
   ____

4. Did you use humor and nonchalance and model self-acceptance in the process? Please explain.

____

____

____

5. Did your staff disclose gifts and challenges as well? Please explain.

____

____

____

6. How much time did you allot for the lesson?

____

For the experience?

____

7. What did you observe regarding the children's response to the Gifts and Challenges experience?

____

____

____

8. Did you prepare the environment/activities ahead of time with extra materials, unusual equipment? Please explain.

____

____

____

9. Did you only make use of the regular classroom materials? Please explain.

____

____

____

10. If you have given this experience more than once or made it a part of your curriculum, what long-term benefits have you noticed in your school culture or with individual students?

____

____

____

11. Have you had separate Challenge Days? Please explain.

____

____

____

12. How have you implemented Challenge Days?

____

____

____

13. Other ideas you wish to implement:

____

____

____

____

____

____

Table 6-4: Teacher's Focus Chart

As a teacher, one of my Gifts is:

____

One of my Challenges is:

____

____

A gift I choose to highlight this week:

____

____

What day will I do it?

____

Where?

____

What will I need? (supplies, space)

___

___

Who will I share with?

___

When?

___

A challenge I choose to highlight this week:

___

___

What day will I do it?

___

___

What will I need? (supplies, space)

___

___

Who will I ask for support or help?

___

___

Who will I share with?

___

When?

___

How did it go?

___

___

Table 6-5: Evaluations after a Gifts and Challenges Day

What gifts did you practice?

____

____

Did you feel encouraged, discouraged, joyful, frustrated, or any other feelings?

____

____

____

Did you experience your gift in a group, with one person, a few people, or by yourself?

____

____

____

Write any other thoughts you would like to share about doing your gifts.

____

____

____

Gifts and Challenges and the Subject of Bullying

Although Gifts and Challenges did not come about as a potential aid to address the problem of bullying, there are many benefits inherent in the program which strengthen the abilities of all students by helping them to understand and deal with this issue.

Once children have a clear understanding of their own gifts and challenges and the commonality involved in this idea, it creates a more level playing field when students think about themselves in relation to each other. Working with Gifts and Challenges builds confidence and compassion through an increased understanding of what it is each student has to offer, what each student has to improve, and the knowledge that everyone has equal value. With this confidence instilled at an early age, it follows that children may be less vulnerable to taunts regarding abilities or skills, and that their general emotional resilience has the potential to be quite strong. With the compassion learned from being a support to someone facing a challenge, or from receiving such support, children can then generalize that understanding to anyone else who has a challenge versus distancing them as objects of contempt.

The incidence of bullying in the classroom will be greatly reduced or eliminated because the erroneous thinking inherent in bullying will be exposed early and be more obvious to children with this kind of training. Inoculated with this basic, yet powerful information, students' ability to assert themselves during verbal confrontations, and to mentally defend themselves from the after effects of put downs or teasing, is greatly enhanced.

The actual experience of exercising your gifts in the company of admiring students or teachers, and coupled with practicing your challenges with a supportive friend, makes for an emotionally balanced classroom atmosphere. In this approach, hopefully no one is hiding with festering negative self-talk regarding their challenges. At the same time, one-upmanship regarding one's gifts is not given room to breed as it is obviously based on the false premise that there are only a select few who are valued.

In addition, once the children themselves are armed with this information, they do not need to rely so heavily on adults to protect them from verbal bullying regarding strengths or weaknesses. Over time, they have the opportunity to gain the understanding and the language to counteract these situations with confidence.

The techniques in the section on Laying the Foundation are also critical components toward ensuring the emotional safety of the classroom. The strengthening of self-knowledge and confidence which comes from a familiarity with these tools can prevent the victim stance that seems to invite the advances of bullying.

These ideas must be taught early, preferably beginning in preschool and continuing in 1st through 3rd grades so that they are given a chance to take firm root in the minds of the youngest learners. The tools the students learn at this stage become second nature as they interact with each other, and can then be individually adapted to situations occurring in the students' later years of school.

Former students who participated in Gifts and Challenges lessons

Section 7: Alumni Perspectives

The question came up as to whether former students would have any recollection of doing the Gifts and Challenges program. We wondered whether they might be using some of these ideas in their lives if they did recall it, and what they might be willing to share. Questionnaires were created for those who are now young adults as well as for some of the young teenagers. Following are excerpts from their responses.

Gaby, 13

It made me feel like there was something to take care of but also reminded me that no one is perfect and that I didn't need to waste my time trying to fix idiosyncrasies that are just part of my personality.

... it helps identify my challenges and helps me overcome them. It also reminds me that you are who you are you can't change anything about that and you're still going to be yourself whether people like it or not.

Natalie, 14

I remember one year I was teaching a couple people how to draw a horse and they were so intent on what I was saying and what I was drawing that it made me feel really good that I was helping someone with one of their challenges.

This is a little saying that I thought of that I like to use.

"A challenge is a gift not yet discovered."

Eduardo, 14

I learned not to get upset when I had trouble with something. I would keep on trying until I got it right.

These lessons have helped me a lot. In 8th grade I had a hard time with Algebra, but I kept trying and now it's a gift.

Ben, 14

I remember always feeling very confident after gifts and challenges days because not only did I get to face my challenges, I got to help someone else face theirs as well.

I think gifts and challenges activities were very beneficial because it taught me how to face a challenge instead of try to avoid it.

I think gifts and challenges is a great idea, and I wish more elementary schools did it.

Nadia, 16

It taught me to have patience, acceptance, and kindness for others. Instead of hiding from our challenges, we would embrace them and realize that they weren't all that bad, and they were just a natural part of life. It was always enjoyable to watch our teachers (Judy and Mel) deal with their Gifts and Challenges. All of the students had different challenges, and one person's challenge was another's gift, so those two would help each other and learn from one another, embracing their Gifts and Challenges with open arms.

The whole experience of Gifts and Challenges opened my mind to being unafraid of my challenges, and that I could do it, if I tried. It increased my confidence level, and it also let me be open to other's people gifts and challenges. It has helped form my view of people and things in the world.

Christian, 19

Each Gifts and Challenges day provided a new opportunity for enrichment, learning, and developing self-esteem and teamwork.

Each Gifts and Challenges day, I would take advantage of both gifts as well as challenges. I would be certain to teach others about things I knew a lot of, or activities I was good at. I've always been one who enjoys sharing my skills and interests with others, and naturally doing so made me feel delighted and fulfilled on Gifts and Challenges days. On the other hand, frustration would arise during the learning curve period when I began a new challenge of mine. Even so, this frustration was a constructive frustration rather than an anger-based frustration and soon subsided when I took the time to see each new challenge I was trying out as an opportunity to grow and develop my physical, mental, or social skills in various ways.

This helps open students' minds to different activities they may never have tried if they had not attempted them during a Gifts and Challenges day…during Gifts and Challenges days, a friend would introduce me to an activity, further increasing my awareness of what interests my friends around me spend their life pursuing.

The greatest lesson I took from Gifts and Challenges was how to teach. Having people around me that are so open to exploring my interests gave me a medium to work with; I just had to develop the method of speaking that would best cater to the individual I was teaching my gift to.

Lauren Yeske, 21

I remember the idea of "talents" making a particular impression on me. As a fairly hardworking child with a few perfectionist tendencies, I liked the idea that we could turn challenges into talents. We don't need to be put off or discouraged by our challenges because perseverance can make us competent and even allow us to excel in areas that were previously difficult for us.

As for gifts, I remember making something for an auction. My sister and I penned the names and a gift of each member of our class on something—a canvas bag, I believe it was. It wasn't difficult to come up with something for each person. That's why I think it was an important exercise. Everyone has gifts, qualities, and abilities, which come naturally to them. Back then I remember it being very clear what I should write about each person.

Our gifts made us unique, and we all had them. It was a way to relate to one another and help us to construct our individual identities. Which of my gifts would I like to define me? How do I choose which gifts to use and which challenges to work on? Will I let my challenges limit me?

I like to think that perhaps the lessons I learned from Gifts and Challenges help me to appreciate my own strengths and weaknesses (it can be difficult to accept our weaknesses and actually allow ourselves to utilize our strengths, I find). Also, though, to appreciate the gifts that other people have.

For example, my most successful friendships are those in which I have accepted the challenges that people have and appreciated their gifts. Being disappointed when a friend shows weakness in an area that I know is a challenge for them is a waste of energy for me and very unfair to them. One of my good friends shies away from confrontation. One of her challenges is articulating what she is feeling and defending herself in moments of conflict. Time and time again I have watched her relationships with other people fray because she dealt with disagreement in a very juvenile manner. I love our friendship and so I am committed to remembering this challenge of hers and being patient when we hit a rocky patch. Luckily, in turn, I get a very loyal friend who also accepts and even shares some of my challenges. I also benefit from her gifts, one of which is her ability to bounce back from a tough situation in a joyful way. Our friendship got better when we worked with each other's challenges and gifts!

Section 8: Comments from Teachers

Amber Hutton, Second Grade

I would say that the idea of Gifts and Challenges is something that I remind my students of all the time. It is not just one lesson, but a lesson that should be taught and instilled in children daily.

Wendy Citron, Montessori Upper Elementary

The Gifts and Challenges program is extraordinary! Each year I find my classroom community coming together through the thought–provoking activities and lively discussions provided by the program. Individual confidence builds through self-awareness as students are asked to take an introspective look inside themselves. The intricately woven lessons set the stage for talking about many differences we face in our lives and bring students closer to help one another identify the similarities that make us all human. Hands down I consider this program to be an integral part of the classroom curriculum.

Julie Macdonald, First and Second Grade

It is through the process of reflecting upon our own individualism that we begin to understand our purpose, as well as our vulnerabilities. "Gifts and Challenges" is a platform that begins this process with students at a very young age, a process that we, as adults, often struggle with.

In using this program in my own first and second grade classroom, I have watched students as they listen to teachers verbalize their own gifts and challenges. This is an enlightening process for students as they see that it's all right to admit what's difficult and ask for help to reach one's goals. The converse is that they become highly engaged as they practice their gifts, losing themselves in the work that is wholeheartedly part of who they are.

"Gifts and Challenges" models the lives of individuals within a larger society. Students begin to come to the realization that we are all interdependent. We may not be good at everything, but we are born with inherent abilities that are the tools for our life's work. People within a thriving community support each other's endeavors, use their own strengths for the betterment of themselves and society, and seek the gifts of others when needed. The same thing can happen in a classroom through the implementation of this program.

Tess Weisbarth, Fifth Grade

Most children are realistic about their strengths and what they need to work on. They also appreciate the opportunity to be asked about those strengths, as well as talk and write about them, and most importantly practice their gifts with their peers. This curriculum makes space in a big part of their world, the school environment, to be open and honest about who they are, what they have to offer, and what others have to offer them.

One year a student was feeling very insecure during the process of sharing her gifts. She was red in the face, watery eyed, and not writing any of her gifts down. When asked if she was okay, she said she didn't know her gifts. Her classmates were so surprised, and within seconds warmly and enthusiastically shared what they observed as her gifts. A big smile crept across her face and her response was, "Oh yeah, that's right." Moments later she was writing a long list of gifts she felt she could share. Her sullenness turned to a sense of pride with having something to offer.

Kathy Schaefer, Montessori Upper Elementary

The children who came into my upper elementary class had been practicing their Gifts and Challenges with Judy for three years. They were well aware of the Comparison Jungle. They rejoiced in opportunities to spend uninterrupted time dedicated to celebrating their gifts and practicing their challenges.

Curiously, as they entered our classroom and a new stage of development, all of this looked and felt a little different. Their sense of self had matured as they became more aware of social expectations and their own place in the social scheme. The children's ability to articulate their feelings and thoughts had also evolved, adding richness and detail to our discussions. It was a student's suggestion that when we had a Gifts morning, they should start in small random groups, demonstrating their gifts to a few peers (not just their best friends) and acknowledging each other. It was a joy to observe the students respectfully watching each other, asking questions and giving compliments, sometimes to someone whom they only knew casually. Then they would all freely and joyfully engage in singing, puzzles, roller skating, cooking, or whatever gift they had chosen. At the end of these sessions, the follow-up discussions were always delightful. Everyone had learned something new and really interesting about someone else. Even after being together for so many years!

My personal favorites were our Challenge days. We'd begin by discussing Challenges, reviewing how they feel and what we want to practice doing about them. Then the oldest children in the class would have an opportunity to name a challenge and ask their younger classmates if someone could help them with it. A time would be set, materials would be gathered by the helper, and, after a little pep talk, reminding both members of a team about how the other might be feeling, they would get busy. These were always, without fail, enormously successful in every way. The follow-up discussions were rich with new confidence, insights about themselves and their friend, and lots of laughter.

The language of Gifts and Challenges was enormously helpful to these children as well. It gave them a non-judgmental way to describe what was happening in their work and their relationships. It was also deeply helpful to teachers when talking with their parents about their child's progress. Everyone was reminded that learning is a lifelong continuum, and we are all works in progress. The importance of each child's supportive words, to their friends and to themselves, is a lesson I hope each of my students will carry for the rest of their lives.

Section 9: The Journals

The first journal (Level 2) was initially designed as a folder to house the charts and as a way for the children to keep track of gifts they would like to exercise and challenges they would like to practice. It also briefly describes the qualities of gifts and of challenges.

As it has evolved, there are now pages included for self-reflection, a spot for drawing yourself exercising a gift, and another spot for drawing yourself being helped with a challenge. The children seem to particularly enjoy the task of depicting themselves in either the gift or challenge roles.

It also contains a list of rights and guides, as well as a place for recording a few inspirational quotes that each child chooses as personally meaningful.

There is also a simplified pictorial journal (Level 1) designed for use by kindergarteners. This is introduced to them in the spring prior to joining the elementary class, with the help of older experienced students. We have also successfully used this version with first grade students.

There is another version of the journal for use with older students (Level 3).

This is a general description of how we are currently using the journals, but there are many creative ways to incorporate them into your own classrooms. I encourage you to experiment.

Journal Introduction

To the Parent or Teacher:

The ideas found in this journal came about when one of my students was comparing himself negatively to another child's progress in a reading workbook. He didn't get there by himself. The innocent, yet insensitive comments of another child only served to heighten what he may have already observed as his placement in the ranking system that seems to spontaneously arise in most classrooms. The depth of discouragement and the sad feelings that this let loose in him struck a deep chord within me as his teacher and because of the love I felt for him as the son of one of my closest friends. The "lessons" in this journal were inspired by the idea that there must be a way to better protect the child's right to learn at the speed and in the way that is most suited to each. In tandem with this thought is that the emotional climate of the classroom as a whole must be strengthened so that it is an encouraging atmosphere for everyone. To me, this meant re-educating and awakening the sensitivity of all my students in a dramatic way. It is my hope that these practices will not only make many classrooms safer places to learn, but that as the children themselves absorb these ideas, they will ultimately become the guardians of their own emotional safety as they continue learning throughout their lives.

Sample pages from Journal Level 1.

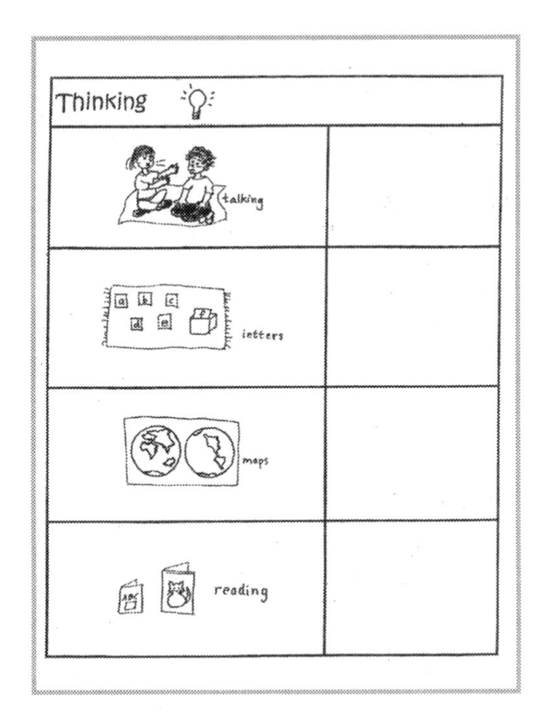

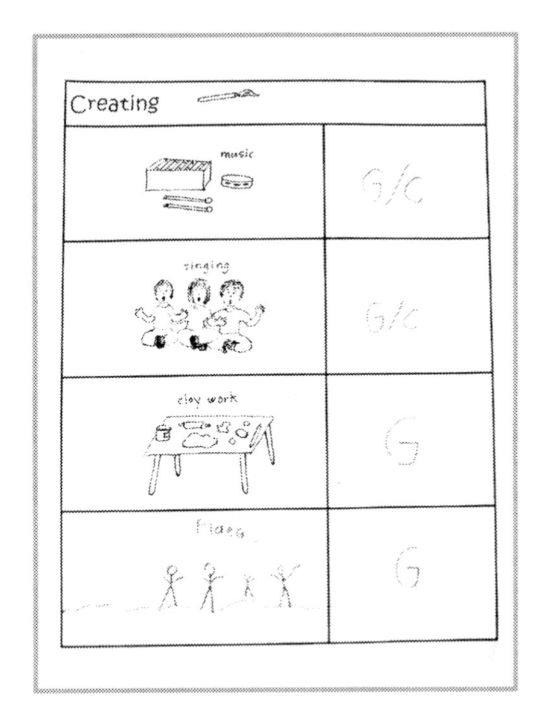

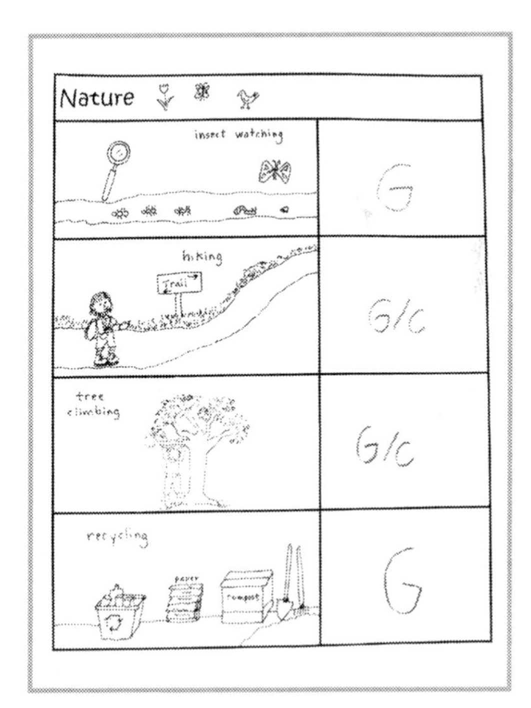

Sample pages from Journal Level 2.

Exercising My Gift

The Gift I am exercising today is:

What do I need to exercise my Gift?

Who will I share my Gift with?

Picture of me exercising my Gift:

drawing

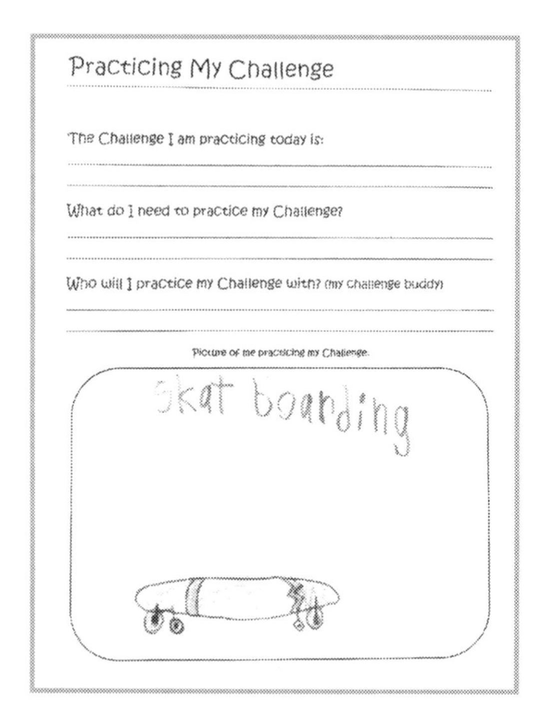

Practicing My Challenge

The Challenge I am practicing today is:

What do I need to practice my Challenge?

Who will I practice my Challenge with? (my challenge buddy)

Picture of me practicing my Challenge:

skat boarding

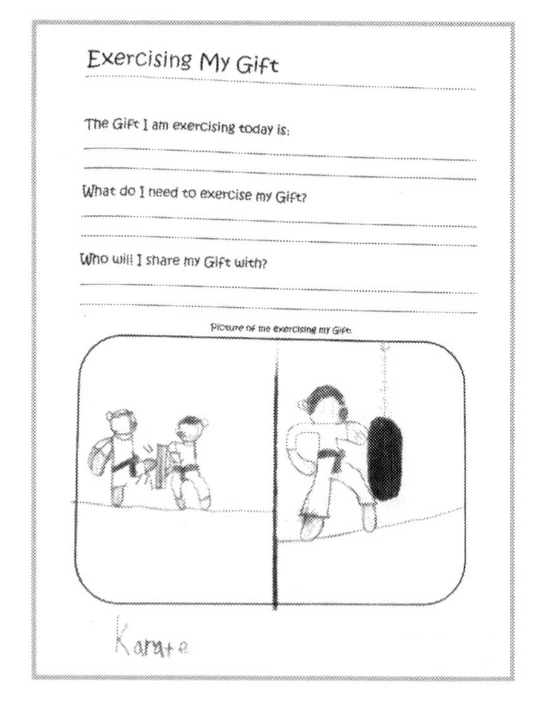

Exercising My Gift

The Gift I am exercising today is:

What do I need to exercise my Gift?

Who will I share my Gift with?

Picture of me exercising my Gift:

Karate

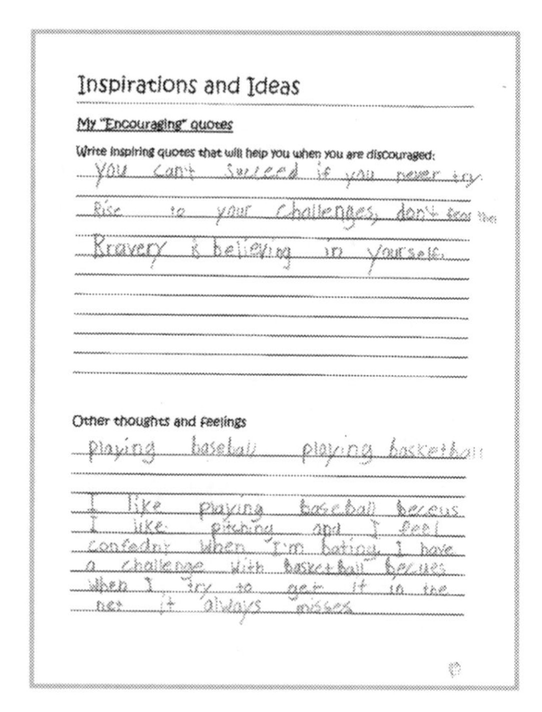

Inspirations and Ideas

My "Encouraging" quotes

Write inspiring quotes that will help you when you are discouraged:

you can't succeed if you never try.

Rise to your challenges, don't fear the

Bravery is believing in yourself.

Other thoughts and feelings

playing baseball playing basketball

I like playing baseball becaus I like pitching and I feel confednt when I'm bating. I have a challenge with basketball becues when I try to get it in the net it always misses

Journal Level 2 sample chart pages.

My Gifts and Challenges

Place a G in front of each item you think is a Gift. Place a C in front of each item you think is a Challenge.

Thinking

- G Reading
- G/C Talking
- G Writing
- G/C Storytelling
- G Remembering
- G Listening
- G/C History
- C Geography
- G Zoology
- G Math
- G/C Botany
- G Science
- G Puzzles
- G/C Riddles
- G/C Connecting ideas
- G Organizing
- G/C Planning
- ____

Creating

- G Drawing
- G Painting
- G Clay work
- G Building
- G/C Singing
- G/C Making music
- G Woodworking
- G/C Designs
- G Art ideas
- G Inventing
- G Weaving
- G/C Sewing
- G/C Constructing
- C Humor
- G/C Acting
- G/C Cooking
- G/C Gardening
- G Poetry
- G Photography
- G Paper crafts
- ____

Body

- C Football
- C Skateboarding
- G/C Basketball
- G Rollerblading
- G Soccer
- G/C Swimming
- G Running
- G Skipping
- G Gymnastics
- G Ice skating
- G Jump roping
- G/C Rhythm
- G/C Dancing
- G Throwing
- G Catching
- G Jumping
- G Hiking
- C Karate
- G Baseball
- I Horseback riding
- G Skiing
- G Bike riding
- G Tennis

Nature

- G/C Bird watching
- G Nature hiking
- G/C Gardening
- G Creating with nature
- G/C Animal tracks
- G/C Nature sounds
- G Rock collecting
- G Tree climbing
- C Animal habits
- G/C Seed collecting
- G/C Animal care
- G/C NSEW directions
- ____

Kindnesses

- G/C Patience
- G/C Generosity
- G/C Thoughtful
- G Helpful
- G Trustworthy
- G/C Encouraging
- G/C Sharing
- G Honesty
- G Respectful
- G Caring
- G/C Loyalty
- G/C Compassion
- G/C Attentive
- ____

People

- G Friendly
- G Peacekeeper
- G Helper
- G Leader
- G Cooperative
- G Bringing people together
- G/C Accepting of others
- G/C Joyful
- G Ideas for activities
- G Calming
- G Problem solver
- G/C Observant
- ____

Some sample chart pages from Journal Level 3.

Thinking

Reading:	Expressive ____	Silent ____	Compre-hension ____
Math:	Computation ____	Base ten/ place value ____	Fact memory ____
	Word Problems ____	Geometry ____	Algebra ____
Talking:	Conversation skills ____	Debating ____	Public speaking ____
Writing:	Creative ____	Essays ____	Persuasive ____
	Poetry ____		
Storytelling:	Humorous ____	Anecdotes ____	Tall Tales ____
Memory:	Myths ____		
	Events ____	Dates ____	Facts ____
	Math ____	Language ____	
Listening:	Stories ____	Directions ____	Facts ____
	Music ____		
History:	Ancient ____	American ____	State ____
	European ____	Eastern ____	
Other:	____	____	____

Creating

Drawing:	Animals ____	People ____	Landscapes ____
	Objects ____	Abstract ____	
Painting:	Animals ____	People ____	Landscapes ____
	Objects ____	Abstract ____	
Clay Work:	Hand Building ____	Wheel Work ____	
Buliding:	Legos ____	Knex ____	Cardboard ____
	Wire ____	Other ____	
Singing:	Reading Musical Notes ____	Memory for Words ____	
	Harmonizing ____	Memory for Words ____	
Musicality:	Playing an Instrument ____	Piano ____	Violin ____
	Guitar ____	Flute ____	Recorder ____
	Harmonica ____	Drums ____	Composing Songs ____
Wood Working:	Constructing ____	Carving ____	
Other:	____	____	____

Kinesthetic Skills

Running or Jogging:	Laps ____	Sprints ____	Track ____
	Distance ____	Cross Country ____	
Roller-Blading:	Sidewalk ____	Park ____	Regular ____
	Tricks ____		
Soccer:	Position ____	Kicking ____	Passing ____
	Goalie ____	Other ____	
Basketball:	Free Throws ____	Lay-ups ____	Passing ____
	Guarding ____	Forward ____	
Baseball:	Hitting ____	Fielding ____	Catching ____
	Running ____	Stealing ____	
Football:	Kicking ____	Running ____	Passing ____
	Receiving ____	Defense ____	Offense ____
Lacrosse:	Catching ____	Passing ____	Throwing ____
	Clearing ____	Cradling ____	Shooting ____
Other:	____	____	____

Nature		Virtues		People Skills	
Bird Watching	____	Patience	____	Friendly	____
Nature Hiking	____	Generosity	____	Peacekeeper	____
Creating with Nature	____	Thoughtfulness	____	Helpful	____
Gardening	____	Helpfulness	____	Leader	____
Creating with Nature	____	Trustworthiness	____	Cooperative	____
Animal Tracks	____	Honesty	____	Organizer	____
Nature Sounds	____	Sharing	____	Tolerant	____
Rock Collecting	____	Kindness	____	Joyful	____
Tree Climbing	____	Respectful	____	Observant	____
Animal Habits	____	Caring	____	Harmonizing	____
Seed Collecting	____	Loyalty	____	Calming	____
Animal Care	____	Compassion	____	Problem Solver	____
North, South, East West Directions	____	Encouraging	____		
		Considerate	____		
Other	____		____		____

PDFs of journal pages, Gifts and Challenges Charts and support materials are available on the Gifts and Challenges website at www.giftsandchallengesbook.com or contact Judy Donovan at donovanhunt@sbcglobal.net.

Conclusion

As teachers we need to encourage students to become individuals who are emotionally literate. Teachers and parents need to create environments for students which will lead to self-compassion and hopefully, compassion for others. The great opportunity of these ideas is the ability to guide those children in our care to become all that their gifts will allow, fully aware of what they have to offer. The equally important hope is that they will rise willingly to their challenges and see in them a great opening for what they may transform in themselves.

Emboldened with the inner strength that these ideas have given them, they will not see their world as a daunting or threatening place, but a fertile and welcoming field in which to sow the seeds of their gifts.

Through the Gifts and Challenges program we immerse children in this kind of self-awareness; we remove the obstacles to initiative and nurture a joyful intellectual empowerment. We promote an attitude of enthusiastic optimism toward learning and its challenges, born of natural and balanced confidence.

Acknowledgments

I would like to acknowledge the work and genius of Beverly Cassell through the Artists Conference Network. The principles in her program have inspired many ideas in my work with children.

I would also like to thank my art mentor, Leigh Hyams, for the brilliance of her teaching and for her embodiment of the idea that creativity is essential in everyone's life.

I would like to thank Randy Keeney for the Comparison Jungle idea, which has become such an important concept in the work and a real help to all the students.

Without the trust, support, and creative freedom afforded by the directors of Sunrise Montessori, Janice Tres and Bonnie Sauer, the development of these ideas would have had no place to grow and ultimately be embraced by our school community.

Kathy Schaefer, my teaching colleague and mentor at Sunrise, was essential in following through in the Upper Elementary when the idea was first presented, and thoughtfully developed the experience to suit the needs of the older child. She respectfully kept the experience going with the students over the three year span of their Upper Elementary education. Her warm and balanced encouragement has been invaluable through all the phases of this project.

Heartfelt thanks belong to my teacher assistant and right hand, Melanie Oftedal, who encouraged and supported these ideas with such enthusiasm from the very first experiment. Her creative suggestions and positive attitude through all the iterations of this work have kept the idea alive and well in our classroom culture.

Additional gratitude goes to all my assistants for their brilliance in helping our students, while exercising their own gifts: Donna Risinger, Paula Teixera, and Patricia Manrique. I would also like to thank Julie Macdonald, my co-teacher for four years, for her own personal contributions to the many Gifts and Challenges lessons that we orchestrated together. In addition, I would like to acknowledge the work of Amber Hutton during our teaching years together, and for the beautiful icon drawings she made for the Needs Wheel. I am greatly indebted for the Peacemaking ideas and beautiful procedures which came directly from the longstanding work done in this area by Montessorian, Ursula Thrush.

Deep appreciation goes to Paulette Harris, my dear friend, who supported and admired the concept from its inception. She acted selflessly as my sounding board and encouraged me through all my versions of self-doubt. She also contributed the idea for the journal, and worked on it for many dedicated hours. Katie Donovan, my sister, has provided steady guidance, insightful suggestions, careful editing, and shepherded this book material through countless versions. Her belief in the project has meant everything to me and undoubtedly helped me stay the course. Her knowledge of social media, combined with her own brilliant writing and laser sharp thinking are contributions so vital to getting the message out into the larger arena. My mother, Mary Donovan, has provided the perfect model of how to stay present and attuned to children and it is to her that I was speaking as I wrote the first draft of the book.

Linda Newstrom-Lloyd is the person who first encouraged me to write these ideas down as if I were explaining them to a friend. Her belief in the concept was essential. Great thanks belong to my fellow Montessorian from Michigan, Pam Nelson and her husband Jim Nelson, who both realized the potential for a book in all these ideas. Regina Krausse and Pam Johnson have both been my longtime friends and coaches. They have generously used the Artist Conference Network coaching techniques that have effectively helped to slice through my negative thoughts around the project to reveal the central vision. This was invaluable in helping me stay in action toward my goals for the book. Tess Weisbarth has been my trusted friend and spiritual supporter throughout the years of this project, trying out the ideas with her students, and persistently nudging me to bring the materials into the larger educational community.

I am grateful to Jane Wechsler, director of Family Montessori School, for allowing me to give one of the first workshops to her teachers. Wendy Citron, a fellow Montessori teacher, has also been so encouraging and consistently and effectively used the material with her students over the years.

Deidre Moore helped contribute to the organization of the book as well as the beautiful refinement of the Feelings and Needs wheels for use in the classroom. Amy Hebert has contributed beautiful photographs of the students as they experienced the Gifts and Challenges lesson. Luke Sauer and Gus Carpenter have done splendid work in filming the students in the process of Gifts and Challenges Days. Luke Sauer edited the film and made the work beautifully accessible for teachers and parents.

Amanda Hallahan has spent many concentrated hours on the book's structure and editing. Her organization skills were so instrumental in taking the papers to the next level, making the project more coherent and readable for teachers. Her optimism and encouraging attitude while working on the book project as well as her enthusiastic help in implementing these ideas in the classroom have been so appreciated.

Great appreciation goes to Annette Gorden for her patience and persistence in the exercise of her wonderful editing talents in bringing this project to its final completion. Thank you as well, to Kathy Merritt, for her diligent and meticulous proof reading of the final draft.

I would also like to thank the alumni students for their written contributions to this book. Knowing that they still remember these lessons makes it all worthwhile. I would like to thank and acknowledge the important contributions of all my students over the years. They have embraced these ideas with enthusiasm and ownership, and added their own brilliant thoughts to the on-going mixture of Gifts and Challenges lessons. They have helped keep the ideas fresh and made an important contribution to the students of the future.

My husband, Lauren Hunt, has been my stalwart companion and ready enthusiast for all the stages of this project. His quiet confidence in me and the material have been the invisible pillars of the building of this work. His patience through the late night hours and physical chaos that making a book generates, gave me the freedom to pursue the inspiration when it came.

About the Author

Judy Donovan is a Montessori-trained teacher who has been teaching in both preschool and elementary levels for 35 years. She has a passionate interest in helping children learn with confidence and balanced self-awareness. While much of her career has been in the private Montessori school setting, she also worked for five years in a public school system.

Judy believes that there is a special call for educators to teach their students emotional literacy and to foster compassion among the students toward themselves and others at any point in the learning process. She believes this will create classrooms that are safe for all types of learners. Her Gifts and Challenges Curriculum will resonate with teachers in both public and private school settings. Parents, too, will find great comfort in the skills their children acquire from this curriculum which will last them a lifetime and make them better citizens of the world.

The Gifts and Challenges Curriculum is more than a series of lesson plans—it becomes a lasting context for a rich and nurturing learning environment. Students learn the skills to celebrate their own (and others) gifts and the tools for thinking and acting differently when faced with their own or others' challenges. Simply put, Gifts and Challenges can create an emotionally safe learning environment and naturally confident students.

The Gifts and Challenges Curriculum was created more than 15 years ago as a spontaneous answer to solve a problem for one student. Donovan learned that this child was deeply hurt by some off-hand comments made by another student which negatively compared this child's progress with their own. The first presentation of the Gifts and Challenges lesson mesmerized the children, capturing their hearts and minds. Since then, the Gifts and Challenges Curriculum has grown and deepened—often with the input and inspiration of the students themselves. Donovan has presented the Gifts and Challenges Curriculum in professional publications and for in-service teacher training events in California.

"I have always seen my role as an advocate for children and their right to learn free from self-doubt," said Donovan. "Perhaps that is why I was so sensitive to seeing the circumstances as a perfect opportunity to do more than just scold a child or two for making some insensitive remarks to a classmate. The children and my role as their champion in the realm of emotional safety served as the inspiration and the fertile ground that allowed Gifts and Challenges to grow."

"In my free time I am an artist and have applied these principles to challenges in my artwork. I have found that the enduring messages from Gifts and Challenges about honoring your gifts and rising to your challenges was not just for the children in the classroom, but really for all of us. My wish for you as a teacher or parent is that you find in Gifts and Challenges an invaluable aid for helping children become the naturally confident learners they were meant to be."

Judy Donovan lives in Napa, California with her husband, Lauren Hunt.

Printed in the United States
By Bookmasters